Ford Taylor has mastered the art of Relactional Leadership. This book provides the foundation that will be a catalyst to personal and cultural transformation in every marriage, family, institution, and organization that embraces and implements its proven principles.

—**STEVE FEDYSKI**, Chief Operating Officer, Pure Flix Entertainment

In *Relactional Leadership*, Ford Taylor has managed to do something that very few have been able to do successfully - to bridge the gap between being relational and still getting results... and all of this in a way that lets people know that they are valued and that their choices are respected. Ford's practical approach will help every leader to become more effective in the home, on the job, or wherever they are in creating cultures in which people are free to flourish in an atmosphere of openness and accountability. Ford is also a pioneer. With the level of organizational disruption that is being created across the globe by the speed and magnitude of technological advance, this is exactly the kind of leadership that will be needed to help to prepare us for the future. It's no longer an option. It's a priority. I highly recommend this book!

—**DR. ARLEEN WESTERHOF**, Founder and Executive Director,
European Economic Summit

Ford speaks authentically, compellingly, relationally, and from both the heart and the mind. It's a delight to me when I see members of our Pinnacle Forum network robustly living out their unique calling, and in writing this book, Ford has done just that. His weaving together life experiences with both affective and cognitive insights is a contribution to the examination of leadership that should not be missed.

—**GUY RODGERS**, President & CEO, Pinnacle Forum

Ford's *Relactional Leadership* is fundamental and foundational learning for leaders to improve the lives of those around us, whether they be employees, customers, or family. It compels us to master the art of leadership by becoming both relational and transactional by our very nature. Ford Taylor's *Relactional Leadership* will be mandatory reading for every manager I ever hire from here on out. A Relactional Leader is the only kind of leader worth following!

—**DR. ROLLAN ROBERTS II**, CEO, The Business Battleground, Inc.

I have had the pleasure of knowing Ford for almost 35 years. The man's life has been changed spectacularly because he has applied the words from this book before he shared them with us. Kudos to Ford and his team for changing so many lives. Dive in and see how they affect you.

—**Peter J. Kubasek**, Managing Partner, ArkMalibu

Ford writes from a base of experience that lends credibility to his words and brings life to his "tools." The Relational Leader is a remarkable set of reality tested tools that allow anyone anywhere in the organization to bring a new level of leadership to the challenges we all face in today's business climate. A must-read for the novice and the expert!

—**Robin Altland**, CEO, Performance Dynamics International

Ford personally took our company through Transformational Leadership (TL) five years ago. As a result, we've seen same-store sales increase over a million dollars each year. Not only that, we have empowered our employees to perform their jobs with renewed energy and excellence because of the tools made available to all the leaders. I am forever grateful to Ford for his comprehensive, intentional, holistic approach to leadership. I can't wait for our team to dive into his new book and see what aspects of leadership we can all learn to employ in both our personal and professional lives.

—**Britney Ruby Miller**, President, Jeff Ruby Culinary Entertainment

Leaders seek to influence others in a positive way, create an impact in the world around them, and find both success and significance. The question I hear from leaders the most is how to succeed at business without losing their family, passion, and heart. In this book, Ford shares exactly *how* to succeed at both with actionable, step-by-step advice and stories that you will love and be able to relate to. You are a leader, you want to make a difference, and you want to build an incredible company while creating deep and loving relationships with those most important to you. This book will take years off of your journey doing just that! Thank you, Ford, for writing this much-needed book!

—**John Ramstead**, CEO, Beyond Influence,
Inc. Magazine's "Top Leaders to Listen to",
Host of the *Eternal Leadership Podcast*

As a branch office manager and leader of a large team of registered representatives and financial advisor representatives, I have read and studied many books on leadership from well-known authors. While I received some good information, none of them gave me the practical tools like *Relational Leadership* has that have dramatically made my work more fun, impactful, and easier to those I serve. A must-read for anyone in leadership!

> —**MICHAEL NEUMANN**, Branch Office Manager, Financial Advisor
> Representative, Transamerica Financial Advisors, Inc.

Ford's tools provide answers to *every* question, opportunity and consistency in *every* area of business and personal life. These tools "fit" our desired culture so much that we have incorporated them in training for *all* employees. Our ROI: "This has helped my marriage, parenting, customer relations…" Priceless! Added bonus: Business and profits have grown! Ford's teachings have been a great tool to get new employees 'on board' with our culture.

> —**MARTHA J. LOGAN**, President, Korrect Plumbing Heating & Air Conditioning

Relational Leadership and its tools and processes are transforming my life as a leader. Far more than a book on leadership theory, this is one of practical application that is a game-changer for the better in every area in which one has influence.

> —**STEVE IVASKA**, Positive Impact Leadership

Ford has done the unthinkable by bringing scholarship and practical principles together in a one-stop work of wisdom. The results of applying what Ford has laid out in *Relational Leadership* will have the undeniable effects of correcting the course of our private and professional lives. This book is a must-read for everyone who cares about the people they love and the work they do!

> —**RICK AMITIN**, Author of *If Only I Had A Dad: Finding Freedom From
> Fatherlessness*, Host of "Rick on Life" on TLB TV, and Founder of RickAmitin.com

This book is a must read for all Type A leaders! I am a recovering transactional leader. Ford is the reason I am now a "relational leader". What is that? Read this book and find out. It will change your life and make your leadership ten times more effective. This is a must read for anyone who wants to be a better leader and improve their relationships at home and work. Great job Ford!

> —**OS HILLMAN**, President, Marketplace Leaders
> Author, *TGIF: Today God Is First*

Many bright, talented, and capable leaders lack the basic tools necessary to lead their people and teams effectively, and their organizations and businesses underperform as a result. At the same time, research reveals that emotional intelligence is one of the greatest indicators for success. Ford Taylor is an authority when it comes to teaching, training, and equipping people from various walks of life with simple strategies that will increase their emotional intelligence and empower them to become leaders who are truly transformational. The principles he unpacks in this book have changed me, and if you take the time to read it, they will change you, too.

—**BRIAN LEE**, National Director, Beta Upsilon Chi, Inc.

Many can bake a cake. A cake that tastes great that people crave is a gift. Ford makes a phenomenal cake! You'll experience this when you read, taste, apply, and share the wisdom within. Relational Leaders are relatable, results-focused, resonating, and rewarding to be around. With Ford, it emanates from real-world successes and failures, bathed in trust, truth, transparency, and a desire to see personal and organizational transformation. The content challenges your contentedness, producing a discontent that must be addressed. Don't assume you understand leadership until you've devoured this book, gone through the Transformational Leadership (TL) training, and disciplined yourself by applying its wealth. This masterwork reveals blindspots and bottlenecks that, when removed, yield transformational results. Be actional and get relational!

—**JOHN BARKER**, Founder, 213Consultancy.com

I have seen Ford Taylor's principles not only explained in this book but lived out at work, home, and play. From his work with companies to non-profit organizations to kids' teams and community leadership groups in multiple countries, I have watched and experienced people becoming better versions of themselves. May you experience a similar benefit in reading and reflecting through these pages.

—**DOUGLAS HOWE**, The Rawls Group, Insignia Foundation

Relational Leadership offers practical tools and processes of effective leadership, resulting in teams that thrive. The easy-to-follow steps will improve relationships and productivity, lower stress and anxiety, and remove constraints that are hindering performance and growth. Ford Taylor has written a must-read for anyone in a position of leadership. Read this book—and learn from one of the best.

—**KENNETH D. LAWSON**, Owner and CEO, C.C. Creations

Impact and influence must come from a foundation of relationship. My relationship with Ford Taylor goes beyond what we've done together and deeply into the foundation of authentic relationship with life-changing evidence. What you'll read in the pages before you is not theory that has little impact; it is life-filled knowledge that has relevant relational credibility woven into its details. Because I have personally witnessed and experienced these truths lived from Ford to me personally, it makes this book a profound document of truth and transformation.

–**Patrick "Paddy" McBane**, Director & Founder, Marketplace Solutions, Consultant, Coach, & Trainer for Transformational Leadership (TL)

Ford Taylor has a unique ability to communicate profound truth in amazingly simple ways! The principles he lays out in this book can transform both your personal and business relationships. Practical steps and processes are based on both solid scientific evidence and good old common sense. If true leadership is defined as charting a course for healthy relationships, sustained productivity, and lasting success, then this book should become an invaluable resource for all who are privileged to read it. I wholeheartedly endorse Ford and this timely message.

–**Larry Whittlesey**, National Director, US Mission Network

At the age of 40, I found myself stuck "in a box" I did not want to be in, despite leading what I thought was a successful corporate and business life (having been part of executive leadership in South Africa of global blue-chip IT companies like Hewlett Packard, Oracle Corporation, and Computer Sciences Corporation and having founded a growing investment services company). The "ingredients, tools, and recipe" that you will find in this amazing book helped me to find personal healing and empowered me to take the steps to rebuild relational trust and unity in my marriage, family, and business life after seven years of unconfessed adultery and unethical behavior. It also opened the door for Maude (my wife) and I to start a new business that focuses on fixing and growing organizations by using the wisdom of *Relactional Leadership* as part of our calling to be catalysts for leadership and economic transformation on the African continent.

–**Patrick Kuwana**, CEO and Founder, Crossover Transformation
Africa Coordinator, Unashamedly Ethical

We have known Ford Taylor for over 25 years, and any time he speaks, we walk away with something of great value. Ford has a brilliant business mind meshed with an uncanny way to explain clearly breakthrough leadership techniques. Anyone wanting to improve their ability to lead others and positively influence people needs to read his book. *Relational Leadership*, through real-life experiences and stories, will give you many "aha" moments to make you a better leader and person. For anyone wanting to have their mind opened from a thought leader and great teacher, this book is a must-read.

—**MARK AND DIANA BAYLISS**

Ford Taylor is a leading authority on individual and team performance. We have utilized Ford's Transformational Leadership principles to move our organization to the next level. *Relational Leadership* is more than just a book; it's a blueprint for meaningful and measurable transformation – for individuals, families, and all types of organizations. Everyone needs to embrace and leverage this powerful "field guide" on their mission of transformation – personally, in the marketplace, or their communities… one relationship at a time.

—**JIM SCHUBERT**, Chief Culture Officer, Pure Flix Entertainment

Ford is the real deal. I have worked, laughed, planned, and seen great victories by his side for years. He is a man committed to the integrity of living what he teaches. These tools are alive, effective, and powerful beyond measure. The world would truly be filled with peace and wisdom if millions of individuals would welcome these tools into their lives. Having worked closely with Ford and seen all aspects of the TL training in motion, I strongly endorse the man and the material. Enjoy, partake, and drink deeply from this well of truth, and you will never be the same.

—**CATHERINE WEBB WILLIAMS**, CEO, FSH Strategy Consultants

If you are interested in practical, actionable ways to navigate and lead in any community setting—be it business, governmental, family, or other arenas that have to do with more than just yourself (i.e. life!)—do yourself a favor and read this book; then, re-read it; then, practice it. *Relational Leadership*, which is a cute way of bringing together the two primary categories that occur in all human interaction—relational and transactional—will provide easy-to-start guidelines. But, like anything real, it must be practiced over and over. Our "relational muscles" have to be trained—much like exercise, learning a foreign language, or learning a musical instrument. But, like these other "real" things in life… it is worth it!

—**ROB STEASE**, Owner, Honeymoon Paper Products

Ford weaves the lessons in this book in such a way that, by the end, the bubble has burst, and you cannot return but instead must move ever-forward "beyond the bubble." As I read through, I identified with quite a number of situations and could not help but stop and apply the lessons with great success, effortlessly. Indeed, these are everyday life nuggets. Thank you, Ford, for again sharing with us how we can transform our lives and thereby transform many lives in our circles of influence and beyond for the greater good.

—**VALENTINE GITOHO**, Co-founder and Chairperson, African Council for Accreditation and Accountability

We have all read many books on leadership. They all seem the same, focusing on how and what to do. So often, the books are focused on the steps to take to success—the transactional side of leadership. But where does relationship fit into all of this? Ford Taylor, in *Relational Leadership*, takes all the best traits of a transactional leader and all the best traits of a relational leader and combines them in a book that summarizes what all the best leaders of the world already know: Relationships are just as important as the transactions. And when you balance them both, you can transform companies, countries, cities, and families.

—**JIM BRANGENBERG**, iWork4Him Radio Talk Show Host

Ford Taylor is the freest man I have ever met. He also happens to be the best leader I have ever met. Today, as we face a global leadership crisis, we need Ford's teaching. Having served with a large ministry for over 20 years now, I have received many excellent opportunities for leadership training. However, after encountering Ford in 2010 and learning his Relacional lifestyle, I have not been the same. For seven years now, Ford and I have walked together and I have witnessed him live out everything he teaches. Not only is Ford's teaching revolutionary, but how he teaches the principles is truly transformative. Our families, our schools, our businesses, our governments, our country, and our world need what Ford delivers in Relacional. I know for a fact if you choose to live the Relacional lifestyle, you'll change the world around you!

—**DEMARICK PATTON**, Cru City Orlando

I feel close to this story; it could have been me and my company. Eight years of practicing the transforming concepts of *Relational Leadership* have had a profound impact on my life, my family, my friends, and my workplace. For me, the most potent learnings have centered around the ideas of TFA and the six-step apology. Outside the Bible, this is the best leadership manual I've read.

—**PIERRE PAROZ**, Chairman, American Micro

Relational Leadership and *Transformational Leadership* is simple... but not easy. It takes intentional, ongoing effort to learn and use the Relational tool kit. To this day, the tools continue to help me identify and prioritize personal and organizational constraints that hold me back professionally and personally. My organization, marriage, parenting, and friendships have all reached new highs because of *Relational Leadership*... and, for that, I'm eternally grateful.

    –**BRYAN KAISER**, President, Vernovis

The ability to lead in cross-cultural contexts in ways that are equally relational and transactional has never been as important as it is today. *Relational Leadership* has provided our international organization the practical tools to lead and influence at the highest level of faith-based and civil governments. These tools not only work but also honor the individual or team!

    –**RAY AND LINDA NOAH**, Co-Founders, Petros Network

Ford Taylor's *Relational Leadership* is distinctly impactful as it takes its place in the canon of leadership literature. In it, Taylor giftedly deconstructs the ingredients of leadership, makes them powerfully plain, and reconstructs them into the masterpiece that is the Relational Leader. *Relational Leadership* presents the truest way to lead yourself, your family, and your business. This book is truly for everyone!

    –**LINDSAY FLEMING**, CDO, Omega ProVision

Ford Taylor's new book, *Relational Leadership*, is worth its weight in gold. In fact, it may be more valuable than gold since the price of gold fluctuates, while wisdom never loses value. Two important keys to life are healthy relationships and effective leadership, and Ford delivers both in this explosive, double-barreled, easy-to-read book which packs quite a kick. Ford's easygoing writing style belays his hard-hitting content. *Relational Leadership* is full of practical, experiential wisdom delivered in a nonreligious manner. The book, like its author, is unpretentious, and does what a good business should. It under-promises and overdelivers. Read it asap. You may even want to read it more than once.

    –**BRUCE COOK, PHD**, Chairman, KCIA
    President & CEO, VentureAdvisers

Living in an age that continually focuses on self-awareness and improvement, there is no end to the books that address this subject. In the midst of the many voices giving advice and counsel, Ford Taylor adds his measured, precise, and pointed voice. Ford is a man who has learned what it means to "walk his talk."

This book, while addressing the familiar topic of leadership, stands in a class of its own. The impact of this book is to be found not only in the wisdom and numerous acronyms that help the reader to remember and apply leadership principles, but to the vulnerable and authentic narration provided by Ford. Ford writes not only of his successes but also his failings. His honesty communicates to the core of our identity, to be accepted despite our strengths and weaknesses. His stories, much like the parables, catch the reader off guard and make us open to hear life-giving principles—principles that live in the land between transactional and relational leadership styles.

If you want to see true change happen in your personal life, your family, or your company, you will not be able to read this book once. I believe you will often return to its pages for direction and advice—advice that will transform the way you live, love, and ultimately create a lasting legacy.

—**GRAHAM POWER**, Founder, Global Day of Prayer and
Unashamedly Ethical

RELACTIONAL LEADERSHIP

WHEN RELATIONSHIPS
COLLIDE
WITH TRANSACTIONS:
PRACTICAL TOOLS FOR
EVERY LEADER

FORD TAYLOR

HIGH BRIDGE BOOKS
HOUSTON

Relactional Leadership
by Ford Taylor

Copyright © 2017 by Ford Taylor
All rights reserved.

Printed in the United States of America
ISBN (Paperback): 978-1-946615-92-3
ISBN (eBook): 978-1-946615-07-7

High Bridge Books titles may be purchased in bulk for educational, business, fundraising, or sales promotional use. For information please contact High Bridge Books via www.HighBridgeBooks.com/contact.

Published in Houston, Texas by High Bridge Books

CONTENTS

Introduction

LEAD **RELACT**IONALLY

IN YOUR ORGANIZATION, what happens when highly *relational* people collide with highly *transactional* people? What happens when people-oriented workers intersect with the task-oriented workers? Stress? Anxiety? Anger? Gossip? Underperformance?

On one end of the relationship continuum are people who are highly relational. For these people, the relationship is the most important part of everything they do.

On the other end of the continuum are people who are highly transactional. For these people, it's not usually that the relationship is not important to them; it's just that getting the job done is far more important.

What would happen if highly relational people had the tools to become more transactional without giving up their natural inclination to be relational, and highly transactional people had the tools to be more relational without giving up their natural inclination for transaction. One of your primary jobs as a leader is to provide these "tools" to your people so they can get along well and get the job done well.

The main challenge in leading people with such diverse personality styles is that *you* also have a default style. But in order for your organization to perform at a high level, it's not enough to rely exclusively on your default style of leadership.

It is important to lead both relationally *and* transactionally. This is called *relactional leadership.*

As you model this relactional approach, the people in your organization—whether two people or many—will become happier and more productive as a result. Relactional leaders produce relactional teams. They cultivate organizations in which the people get along well *and* get the job done well. In order for this transformation to start happening in your organization, it must begin with you, the leader.

Yes, *you* are a leader. If you have influence with at least one person, that makes you a leader. And when two or more people are in relationship, that makes an organization. So, if you have influence with at least one person in any organization, this book is for you.

The Tools, Ingredients, and Behaviors of Relactional Leadership

As I have travelled to many cities and countries around the world, I have found that nearly everyone I meet is smart, gifted, or talented in at least one area—often, in multiple areas. I have also found that nearly every person I have met has a huge heart. So, years ago, I started asking myself, *If so many people are smart, gifted, or talented and are also good-hearted, why are these not the sort of people we hear about in the media more often?*

As I wrestled with this question, I began to realize that many have never been given the *who, what, when, where, why,* and *how* of leadership. Most have been given the *what,* but few have been taught the practical tools and processes of effective leadership. I then realized that leadership is like baking a cake.

Baking a cake requires different ingredients, tools/utensils, and a recipe manual. Also, in the best-tasting cakes, there are many ingredients that don't taste good on their own as well as others that do. But, for some reason, when they are mixed together in the right proportions in the right way and cooked at the right temperature, the cake tastes really good.

Leadership is like that. When leaders have the tools, ingredients, the right recipe manual, and an understanding of the process (the "how"), they can lead and influence at levels they never thought possible.

Many leaders have been taught how to manage people, yet few have been taught the practical tools, ingredients, and behaviors to lead people and manage the processes, policies, systems, and procedures around them effectively. This book will help you to acquire these tools, ingredients, and behaviors needed to become a relactional leader who can develop teams that thrive relationally and transactionally.

In the following story, you'll see how the tools, ingredients, and behaviors of relactional leadership converged in action to turnaround a struggling company. As you read, pay close attention to the areas in **bold** lettering. These are many of the tools, ingredients, and behaviors you'll learn about as you journey through this book.

Relactional Leadership in Action

My company was brought in to fix and turnaround a company that was losing approximately $250,000 per month. We were asked to speak with their bankers because their bankers were planning to shut them down. They asked us, "What do you do that's different from what other people do?" This is somewhat difficult to explain because many people believe that what we're doing is only the "soft side" of business. They don't realize how much it impacts the "hard side" and how combining the two increases profitability.

The two owners explained to me, "The bank told us, if we aren't successful in turning our company around, they're going to lock the doors in seven weeks. They told us that, if we use you and don't get it turned around, that's what's going to happen. If we use their people but don't get it turned around, they'll give us more time. What would you do?"

Candidly, I said, "I would use their people. That's the safest thing you can do."

While I was in the office, they called the bank and said, "We've made a decision. We're bringing in Ford Taylor and his team."

When we started this transformation process, this company's team was highly dysfunctional. It was a family-run business, but the family didn't get along. The employees didn't get along. There wasn't a clear vision. There was no **safety** when we walked in the room. Again, we only had seven weeks to turn things around.

First, we established a **social covenant** to build safety and trust as well as to hold people accountable if they didn't act the way we agreed to act. We made sure people understood how to host a meeting using the **W.A.D.E.L. model**. We made it clear that everyone's **feedback** would be valued as we moved forward. We taught about **anger** and helped the company's CEO to understand that his anger was a big problem for the company. The people didn't feel like they could share **feedback** with him. He started learning how to go **silent** when his anger surfaced.

As we began the work, we had to have a **shared vision**. That vision was to turn the company around in seven weeks. This meant we needed to **identify the biggest constraints** in the company before we could move forward. We couldn't just deal with the **symptoms**. We had to confront the issues that were making the most significant impact. These things are extremely difficult to do when people don't feel **safe**. If they don't feel safe to bring up the big issues, they will only talk about the easy stuff.

The people began **affirming** each other. They began talking about their **hippocampus issues** and how those issues were making this turnaround more difficult.

They were walking out the social covenant. I could tap on the CEO's table or on his leg when his anger would come out. He was embracing the practice of **T.F.A.**: "Change the thought. Change the feeling. Change the action." So, he would go silent rather than expressing his anger in counterproductive and destructive ways.

Previously, this company's sales had been decreasing, their costs were going up, they were losing customers, and the bank was about to close them down. Because of the **safe environment** that had been created, we could start asking, "What are the biggest problems here?" We identified that their cash flow was a problem. Their prices were a problem. Their **culture** was a problem. Their lack of **communication** was a problem. Their lack of a **clear vision** was a problem. The sales and production departments didn't get along. Unprofitable sales and unfulfilled delivery promises were being made repeatedly.

I believed the number one constraint was lack of cash flow. Seldom do people consider poor cash flow to be their organization's biggest constraint. Desperate for improvement, they asked, "How do we deal with that?"

I said, "Bring a complete list of all your inventory to me." As I started looking at their inventory, I said, "You have to start selling this inventory even below what it cost you to make it." That recommendation was confusing to them; in fact, it blew their minds. At the same time, they had already absorbed all those costs. They had already spent that money. It made no sense not to move the inventory. They needed the money. When they started doing this, the cash flow problem was corrected.

Then, I started looking at their prices and realized they had been selling things too cheaply. I said, "Can I meet with some of your customers?"

Before we arrived to meet with a customer, I said to the executive team of the company, "Do you **trust** me?"

They said, "Yes."

I said, "Because I'm going to say some things today to your customers that you may not like at first."

We went into the room with the leaders of this $12 billion company that bought from this $21 million company. As we were visiting, the first thing we did was to work through the

W.A.D.E.L model. They weren't used to that. I began by saying, **"Tell us something good."** As we moved forward in the meeting, I explained, "Thank you for meeting with us today. I know you're extremely busy. And I know that you realize this company is not performing well. I understand that they're asking for a higher price than you desire to pay."

They soon asked me, "Why are you here?"

"Well, it's really **simple**," I said. "I have two folders in my hand. This folder is the guidance for how to shut this company down. This other folder is the guidance for how to fix it. If you don't need them in business or don't want them in business, we'll have to shut them down because we can't make it without your help."

Fortunately, no one on our management team gasped aloud or had a heart attack. They stayed in the game.

The representatives of this large company responded by laughing, and one of them said, "We do want them in business."

I said, "Then, can we talk about *this* folder?"

"Yes," they said.

"Here's the thing... We cannot continue generating these products at this price. We have no choice but to ask for a price increase."

They said back to me, "They've been asking for a price increase for 18 months. Why would you get it today?"

I said, "Because I think what they've been asking for is too much."

"What do you think we ought to be paying you?"

"Based on all the evaluations," I explained, "I believe this price [I gave the price] is the right one."

They said, "We'll do that. That's one penny different than what we're paying everybody else."

I said, "Another thing is they owe you about $400,000 on rebates, but they can't afford to pay it. They'll never be able to pay this back and stay in business. I'm going to ask you to forgive those rebates."

They started laughing. The CFO looked at me and said, "Done. We've already written them off." Smart people like doing business with smart people, so they did whatever was necessary to maintain the relationship.

See the difference in the **trust** that comes from being **honest and direct**? The results are much different than merely dealing with the symptoms. When dealing with the real constraint or problem, the symptoms start taking care of themselves.

We went back to our company and started to produce new products that would be sold at the higher prices.

Two days later, they showed me another product they hadn't shown before that had the same pricing issue. I had to call that same customer and say, "I am really embarrassed, but I could use your help on another product, too." They approved that price increase as well.

This team now trusted me, they were starting to trust each other, our prices had increased, and we had some extra cash flow.

At this stage, we could **clearly define each role** and who needed to fill those roles. This increased trust even more.

We now had the CEO **speaking last** in the meetings. He was no longer the one who was demanding everything.

The team now knew how to **deal with upset customers.**

They had learned how to deal with their **upset co-workers** through techniques such as the T.F.A. reminder in meetings.

About a month into the process, they got a call from the banker saying, "We're going to close you down." They were going to shut this company down even before the seven-week deadline they had originally given to them.

They asked me to speak with the banker, and I agreed. The banker called and, over the speakerphone, said, "Guys, you know I'm calling with some bad news."

They said to the banker, "Before you give us the bad news, would you give Ford just a minute to speak?"

"Yes," he said.

I walked him through specifically what we had done over the past four weeks and how we had added about $2.5 million to the bottom line annually and how, over the next four weeks, we could produce approximately that much again if they would just give us another month.

The banker went dead silent. We thought we had lost the connection. This was the banker who told them our way wouldn't work. You could have heard a pin drop.

He came back on and repeated everything back to me. "You're telling me that you got these price increases, you've sped up delivery this much, and you have the people on the team wanting to work together?"

I said, "Yes, that's what's going on right now. And they now have a plan to add this much more to the bottom line over the next month. The team in this company is really strong. They just got on the wrong path and are now on the right path."

He called back a few minutes later and said, "We're going to give you those four weeks."

About a week later, he and his bosses came to visit from two different towns. They met with us and said they had just found an additional $1 million of losses as they were evaluating their books that they didn't know anything about. So, it was actually much worse than anyone had thought. When these top guys from the bank came in, they said, "You realize we're here to take your keys."

Using the W.A.D.E.L. model, I asked them to tell us about themselves. One of them happened to be a deer hunter. Well, I happened to have been a deer hunter earlier in my life, so I started talking to him about deer hunting. Many people would say, "This stuff won't work with bankers. Why would you talk to him about deer hunting?" I talked to him about deer hunting because I wanted to establish a **relationship on common** ground so we would have something in common as we moved into what I knew was going to be a difficult conversation.

In the middle of the meeting, I asked our clients if they would allow me to speak with the bankers alone. It took a lot of trust to walk out of the room and let the consultant talk to the banker who had just said, "I'm taking your keys." In that moment, I knew we had transitioned into **stage four** or maybe even **stage five** as a team.

I looked at the banker and said, "Before you say anything, I have a question for you."

He said, "You all just told me the CFO's gone and that he resigned. Come on. Be honest. You fired him; didn't you?"

I said, "No, we didn't. I promise you we didn't."

"That kind of mistake?" he said. It was a million-dollar error on the balance sheet.

I said, "We didn't have to. He resigned. I'm not going to be dishonest with you."

"Would you have fired him if he hadn't resigned?"

I said, "That's not my responsibility. You'll have to ask the CEO about that."

Now, I knew the answer, but I didn't have to answer it.

I looked at him and said again, "Can I ask you a question?"

He said, "Yeah."

"Why now? After all this improvement, knowing we're right on the edge. Why would you take those keys today? I don't understand. If you'd taken them seven weeks ago, I would have agreed with that decision 100 percent. I would have thrown them to you. But now, you're going to take away 250 jobs after all this improvement? Can you just help me understand that?"

After a lengthy conversation of questions and answers, the guy said, "You know what? We're not going to do it. We're going to give you a couple more weeks."

Within that seven-to-eight-week period, that company went from losing approximately $250,000 a month to making approximately $250,000 a month through **solving constraints,** understanding **role clarity,** understanding how to put a **discipline**

model in place, a **social covenant**, and understanding how to treat one another. The team understood that they had to be **profitable.** As the relational side and the transactional side were working together in this company, the team had become **relactional,** which was moving them into **continuous improvement.** Now, that team could work together. They could do their teambuilding together. They started providing more **training** for their employees.

There was approximately a $500,000-per-month improvement to the bottom line of this $21 million company. Because the company was making money, approximately 250 people got to keep their jobs.

For the first time in his life, the CEO of the company got to hear from his 80-year-old father, "I love you, Son. And I'm proud of you."

As you apply what you read in this book, you're going to acquire the tools, ingredients, and behaviors that can help you to lead relationally, develop relational teams in every sphere of influence in your life, and experience the tangible and intangible rewards that will result. This is **transformational leadership** at its finest.

Part 1

RELACTIONAL THINKING

1

BECOME A BUBBLE JUMPER

DO YOU STRUGGLE WITH CHANGE? I, too, once struggled with change. There was a time in my business and my marriage when I thought I knew it all. It was hard for me to receive constructive feedback, especially if I felt it was critical of me—as I often did. By not being able to receive feedback, it was hard for me to change. I had a *need* to be right *all* the time.

There was a time in my life when I lived in College Station, Texas but was commuting to Cincinnati, Ohio nearly every week. I was gone 50 out of every 52 weeks each year. I would leave on a Sunday afternoon at about 4 p.m., drive a couple of hours, get on an airplane, fly to Ohio, and get back home at about midnight on Friday night. Every once in a while, I'd be lucky and wouldn't leave until Monday morning at 4 a.m. instead of Sunday afternoon.

After months of doing this, one night, I returned home to Texas at midnight. The house was dark. As I was walking through the house and into my bedroom, I heard this little six-year-old voice say, "Hi, Daddy. Can I sleep with you tonight?"

I looked over and said, "Hey, Sweetie." I gave her a kiss and said, "I'll be right back. I'm going to brush my teeth."

When I came back, I told her, "You can sleep in here tonight if you want to." As my head was about to hit the pillow—and it usually takes me a good 5-10 seconds to fall asleep—my daughter said, "Daddy, can we have a snack?"

Because I had been traveling a lot and didn't feel I was being a good father or husband, I was experiencing a lot of guilt at that time. My kids probably could have asked for anything that we could have afforded, and they would have gotten it. And I clearly could afford a snack. So, we got out of bed and walked through the family room and into the kitchen. I asked her, "What would you like to eat?"

She said, "Let's have ice cream."

That was strange because she didn't like ice cream. But if you put a hundred foods on the table along with ice cream and forced me to choose one, it would be ice cream. As I was fixing two bowls of ice cream in the kitchen, I looked back into the family room and saw my six-year-old daughter go to the corner and turn on the television. Then, I watched her take two swivel recliners and turn them sideways. She took two kitchen chairs and slid them right up to the edge of the family room while the chairs were in the kitchen so we could see through the turned recliners.

The two of us sat there in those kitchen chairs with our feet in the family room, watching ESPN on television after midnight through the swivel recliners. I was eating my ice cream and was savoring the moment. I was thinking, *I'm going to get another bowl of ice cream because she doesn't even like ice cream.* I looked over and saw her twirling her spoon around in her ice cream.

After a few minutes of me eating my ice cream and my daughter swirling hers around in her bowl, she asked me with her little voice, "Daddy, can I ask you a question?"

I said, "Sure, Sweetie. You can ask me a question any time you want."

She said, "Daddy, you know that thing that you're doing in Cincinnati?"

"Yes?"

"Did you offer to do that, or did somebody ask you to?"

I looked at her and said, "Well, somebody asked me to."

She never looked up. She kept swirling her ice cream. After a few seconds, she said, "Daddy, do you think you could get them to ask somebody else?"

I had always heard about "alligator tears" and "swallowing an orange." In that moment, I had those alligator tears, and I felt myself swallowing that orange. Here was my six-year-old daughter saying to me, "Daddy, we need you at home."

After I had regained my composure, I replied to her, "Well, you know, Darling... If Daddy wasn't up there helping those people, a lot of people wouldn't have jobs."

That little girl never looked up. She just said, "Then... that's okay, Daddy."

The truth was I had to take that feedback as relevant. I had to decide whether I would keep doing what I had been doing.

At this time, the corporate board had been trying to influence me to move to Cincinnati, but that was not a decision to be made lightly.

The next day, I met with my wife, Sandra, and said to her, "Honey, we have a choice to make. We can either move our corporate office back to Texas, move ourselves to Ohio, or I can quit and do something else. Because what I'm doing is destroying our family."

My daughter's feedback was highly relevant, I had to acknowledge it, and I had to take responsibility for making the necessary changes.

If you decide to go down this trail, you'll be surprised where such good, solid feedback will come from. Maybe even from a six-year-old girl.

If my wife had said something to me like that back then, my anger would have flared up, and I would have said something like, "I'm working hard and making a lot of money. You have a great lifestyle. Why would you ask me that?"

Over time, I have learned two important lessons: 1) *all personal feedback is relevant* and 2) *change seldom occurs until the pain of staying the same exceeds the pain of changing.*

Bubble Jumping

Most of us would agree that we all have a certain way of thinking. We've been taught our whole lives that our own way of thinking is thinking "inside the box." Most of us have been told many times that we need to learn to think "outside the box." I contend that this doesn't work.

When we're in a box (our way of thinking), we may hear or see something that encourages us to make a change. We are encouraged, and we decide to attempt to get outside of that thinking and make a change. But when we get outside of our box, we get uncomfortable and inevitably *crawl* back into our box. We don't just go back; we *crawl* back in.

Later on, we hear something that encourages us and think, *I can do this!* So, we step out to make a desired change, but it gets uncomfortable again.

Once again, we crawl back into our old box, our old way of thinking and behavior.

I contend that your thinking must change *before* you leave your box. You must make a decision and accept that it is going to get uncomfortable. The thought before you leave the old box must be, *It's going to get uncomfortable, and when it does, I am not going to crawl back into the box.* Make the decision. And before you leave your box, make sure your bumper buddies are going to be there to make sure you don't crawl back in. (You'll learn about *bumper buddies* later on in this book.)

If you stay outside that box long enough, you'll find that you'll start to see that box from a different vantage point. You'll move away from that box, but you'll be able to put the good things from that box in your pockets and take them with you while leaving the not-so-good things and behaviors behind. You'll see that you're no longer *inside* or *outside* the box; you're *beyond* the box. That's where you realize it would be just as uncomfortable to crawl back in as it is to keep moving forward.

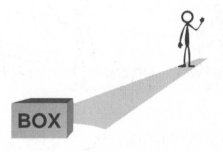

If you stay beyond the box long enough, you will have a brand new way of thinking. This is thinking *beyond the bubble*. A bubble is formed when the pressure on the outside is exactly equal to the pressure on the inside, and the bubble will inevitably burst when the pressure changes. At some point, every bubble is going to burst. So, if we are thinking in a bubble, we know that the pressure on the outside or the pressure on the inside is eventually going to change. This happens on an individual level as well as in our organizations.

In preparation for the bursting of your bubbles, it will help you to expect the unexpected. Unforeseen things will inevitably come at you. If you will learn to accept this reality, it will be easier for you and your organization to move through them and past them in a much better way.

And when the bubble bursts, we cannot return to it because that bubble no longer exists. We must transition into a new bubble. This is what I call "bubble jumping."

I'm sure you've heard the term *paradigm shift*. This is what happens as we go bubble jumping. We're now in a new bubble. Later, in that new bubble, the pressure on the inside or outside may change again. When it does, we will move into a new bubble but won't be able to revert back to that old behavior and way of thinking.

Transformational leaders learn to think beyond the box. They decide to get uncomfortable, leave the box, and refuse to return to the box. They then become bubble jumpers.

Let me share with you another example of a time when I had to start thinking differently in order to experience a desired change in my life.

Over time, I have lost hundreds of pounds, but I would always put the weight back on. Why? When I was thinking inside the box, I would eat a certain way, and I would say to myself, *I'm going to go on a diet.* (People who know me would accuse me of having a sweet tooth. I tell them they're completely wrong; I have 32 of them!)

When I would get outside the box, I would say to myself, *I'm not going to eat! I'm not going to eat!*

But when I was always thinking about "not eating," what was I thinking about all the time? Food.

When we think about what we're not going to do, we eventually crawl back in the box and do exactly what we said we weren't going to do because it's exactly what we've been thinking about.

Once I learned this concept, I changed the way I thought. Instead of thinking, *What am I not going to do*, I started thinking, *What am I going to do*? I started thinking about what I was going to become. I started thinking about becoming healthier. I started thinking about what I would look like and how much better I would feel. Suddenly, I had moved not just outside the box but beyond the box. No longer was I thinking about not eating the pecan pie or the ice cream. I was now thinking about eating healthy food.

Since discovering this principle in late 2007, I have lost approximately 50 pounds. Today, I'm still maintaining that weight through exercise and being careful about how much I feed into those 32 sweet teeth.

We all have a default approach to leadership. As you seek to adapt your leadership style to the needs of each challenge—simultaneously employing both a relational and transactional approach—you'll start jumping into some new bubbles in your thinking. This bubble jumping will result in positive outcomes for yourself as well as for those you influence.

2

THOUGHTS DETERMINE BEHAVIORS

TAKE A MOMENT to read this letter:

> To my family...
>
> As I sit and write this letter, I am in the deepest despair of my life. For the past two years, I have driven to the bridge of the river and contemplated jumping. And sat with a loaded gun many times. Today, as I sit in this chair afraid to go outside alone, knowing that I have done things that are unforgivable, I know it is time to go. I am sorry for the things I have done that have destroyed our future.
>
> Please know that I have called, and the two-year exemption on suicide for my life insurance policy has passed, so I am fully covered. Honey, you and the kids will be completely taken care of financially, and you can be free to find the man that you deserve and a much better father for our children. I will leave the house to do this so it won't cause so much trauma.
>
> I hope that you and the kids can one day find the place in your heart to forgive me. Please pray for my soul, for it may be lost forever.

Question: What are you thinking right now? What was going through your mind as you read that letter? Here are some thoughts you may have had:

- "That poor wife…"
- "Those poor children…"
- "That poor man…"
- "That selfish man…"
- "I've had that feeling before…"
- "I've had this happen in my family…"
- "Why would Ford share a letter like that in a book about leadership?"
- "Is this Ford's letter?"

What you were thinking caused some feelings to arise in you. You may have felt compassion, sadness, empathy, emptiness, anger, or some other feelings. Those feelings were a result of what you were thinking.

Why did I want you to read that as part of a leadership book? There are two reasons.

First, I shared this letter because the rate of suicide around the world is growing at an alarming rate. And those who are struggling with thoughts of suicide feel very alone and ashamed. And when something has a stigma on it like suicide, we avoid talking about it. In addition to suicidal thoughts, other problems—such as cutting, sexual abuse, eating disorders, and others—are systemic in nature and cause millions of people to feel isolated and ashamed. Such epidemics will continue to grow unless we, as transformational leaders, step up and say, "Enough is enough." Those of us who've experienced some of these stigmatized issues must take courage and speak up. People need to know they're not alone and that they can talk about it. The good news is that some people are starting to talk about these painful issues rather than remaining silent amid their hurt.

The second reason I shared the letter above is to help you gain a better understanding of how our brains work. I wanted you to take an inventory of what you were thinking as you read that letter and recognize the feelings that were generated.

In the moment when one of our senses becomes activated—whether through seeing, tasting, smelling, hearing, or touching—a thought occurs. From that thought, a feeling is generated. And from that feeling, an action, reaction, or behavior is chosen.

But if you change the thought, you can change the feeling that results. And if you change the feeling, you will respond with a different reaction or behavior. If we change the behavior, we can get different results; then, we can create a different culture, relationship, or organization.

But if we keep *thinking* the way we've always thought, we're going to keep feeling the way we've always felt. If we keep *feeling* the way we've always felt, we're going to keep behaving the way we've always behaved. And if we keep *behaving* the way we've always behaved, we're going to keep getting the same outcomes we've always gotten.

Personally, I don't want the outcomes I used to get. I don't want the outcome of my marriage not being good due to my unfaithfulness, anger, or passive-aggressiveness toward my wife. Instead, I want the outcome I have now. But I had to change my thoughts, which changed my feelings... which led to new behaviors... which then led to new and better outcomes.

Was that my letter? Yes. Though, I wrote that letter after I decided not to go through with it because I never wanted to forget what that feeling felt like. I wanted to be able to look back and remember it so I would never let myself sink to that place again.

Before we can lead relactional teams, we must become relactional leaders who can facilitate the transformation of organizations. This begins with how we think. And remember that an organization is anytime two or more people are in relationship. And if you have influence with at least one person, that makes you a leader.

The Hippocampus

All the information we take in during our lives is received through our brain stem and a couple of other parts of our brains. Our brains park this information at the doorway of something called the *hippocampus*. *Hippocampus* is the Greek word for "seahorse" because it's shaped like a seahorse.

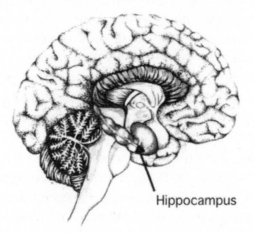

Hippocampus

If information arrives at the doorway of the hippocampus with passion or emotion plus purpose or meaning, that little "seahorse" will open and receive that information.

As this process happens with the same information over the course of our lives, that information will then enter our cognitive memory. Once it gets into our cognitive memory, it will never go away.

When something gets stored in the hippocampus, we are pre-programmed to expect that certain outcomes will result from certain actions. Therefore, many of the responses of people around us—even our own responses—sometimes, don't make rational sense. This is because we respond based on the expected outcome instead of what actually just happened or what was said. Our brains automatically jump to the assumption that we will get the same outcome that we got in the past when those same kinds things happened or were said.

Just as you have stuff in your hippocampus, recognize that those with whom you work also have things in their hippocampuses, too.

Let's imagine you said something to someone in your organization who responded with an extreme knee-jerk reaction that left you wondering, *Where did that come from?* There's a high probability that you said a certain familiar word, you look like someone familiar, you're wearing familiar clothing, or the situation was familiar to a scenario that played out in that person's life when he or she was much younger. That person's brain couldn't process what was happening, so he or she overreacted out of fear of being hurt in the same way he or she was hurt in the past.

It's neither the things we've done in our lives nor the things we've had done to us that prevent us from becoming great leaders. Rather, it's the lies associated with those things that hinder us from reaching our potential. What would happen if we could remove the lies in the hippocampus and replace them with the truth?

When I felt I was supposed to start doing *Transformational Leadership* training, my first thoughts were, *Who would ever listen to me? Look at what I did to my wife. Look at how I was sexually abused at six years old. No one would ever listen to me.* These thoughts were coming from my hippocampus. If I had listened to my hippocampus, this book you're reading wouldn't exist. I wouldn't have started teaching others how to have some successes and how to overcome failures. It was a lie that no one would listen. It wasn't what had happened in reality, nor was it what would eventually happen.

Oswald Chambers said, "There is always one fact more in every man's case about which we know nothing."[1] I say it this way: "There is always one more thing in a person's hippocampus that we know nothing about, and there is always one more thing in your hippocampus that you know nothing about." If someone is responding in a way that could cause you to act inappropriately, remember that there's always one more thing about the pre-programming in that person's hippocampus that you know nothing about. If you can achieve this thinking, your reactions to others will change, and you will have greater and more positive influence than you have ever dreamed of.

Self-Identity

Whether as a leader or a follower, one's *self-identity* consists of what he or she believes to be true about himself or herself. It is made up of three major categories: personal experiences, social comparisons, and internalization of others' judgements. Let's explore these.

1: Personal Experiences

First, our self-identity is shaped through our *personal experiences.* This means that our perception of ourselves is, in part, shaped by the events of our lives.

It's highly possible that we all have some lies running through the filter of our hippocampuses that might have been poured into our self-identities. Perhaps, these lies may have originated from an elementary school teacher, a coach in school, a parent, a sibling, an aunt, an uncle, or a boss. At some point, someone probably said something to each of us that we believe to be true although what was said was a lie.

Let's say that you see me in the grocery store, and you know me. Two of my young daughters are with me, both of whom are under six years of age. One of them is on one side of me, and one's on the other. You come up to me and say, "Hey, Ford!" You then look at one of my daughters and say, "Wow! You sure are pretty!" And you look at the other daughter and say, "You're so sweet!"

What could have happened is, if both of my daughters re-play that scene over and over, one will believe she's pretty but not sweet. The other daughter will believe she's sweet but not pretty.

These sorts of life experiences go on every day of our lives. As leaders, we're doing this to other people, and it's also hap-pening to us.

2: Social Comparisons

Second, our self-identity is shaped by *social comparisons*. These are the thoughts we believe to be true about ourselves as we compare ourselves to others.

Now, let's stay in that same grocery store. Have you ever gone through a checkout line on your knees? Have you ever seen what little children look at? It's pouring into their self-identities. They look to the right and see candy and gum. They look to their left and see all kinds of magazines. They see maga-zines with people who pay a lot of money (many of them) to get to look that way. So, from a very young age, they're thinking, *I'm supposed to eat this and look like this.* And they start comparing themselves to what they see on that magazine. This is what I mean by *social comparison*.

3: Internalization of Others' Judgments

Third, our self-identity is shaped through our internalization of others' judgments. In other words, we decide what to believe about ourselves based on what we "think" others "think" about us.

Have you ever presented something at a meeting or given a talk and, after you finished, you thought, *How did that sound? Did I do okay? Did I say what I wanted to say?* Your answers to these questions are shaping your self-identity.

Are there any things you believe to be true about yourself, either positive or negative, that may not be true? Write down any areas of your self-identity that you believe to be true about yourself that, if you really thought through them, you'd discover they're not true.

Later in this book, you'll learn how *bumper buddies* can help you to identify what you believe about yourself and to help make sure that you are believing the truth.

As you are pursuing the truth about yourself, recognize that all those with whom you have influence are filtering information through the lens of their hippocampus as well as their self-identities.

Changing Your Thoughts

How can we change something in our thought process that we might want to change?

List some of the positive thoughts you have about yourself, and dwell on those for a moment. Focus on one of those thoughts. What feeling do you get when you think about that thought?

Now, ask yourself, "Whenever I feel this way, how do I act? How do I behave? How do I impact the people around me when I'm feeling this way?"

Repeat this process with one of the negative thoughts on your list. How does that negative thought make you feel? Then, ask yourself, "Whenever I feel this way, how do I act? How do I behave? How do I impact the people around me when I'm feeling this way?"

How can you reduce those negative thoughts? How can you shift the negative thoughts into positive ones? The more you think positively on a daily basis, the more you'll feel positively. Your positive feelings will result in more positive actions. Your positive actions will create more positive impact and outcomes for that which you are aiming to influence.

3

DIFFERENCES BETWEEN MEN'S AND WOMEN'S BRAINS

HAVE YOU EVER NOTICED that, sometimes, it's hard to communicate with people of the opposite sex? Let's talk about the difference between men's brains and women's brains. Before we begin, I should preface this discussion by saying I'm speaking in general as these generalizations don't apply to every man or woman. The point of this chapter is to point out the challenges we face in communicating with people who are different than we are.

If I had to draw a picture to illustrate how a woman's brain works, I would just scribble all over the page. Generally speaking, in a woman's brain, everything is connected to everything. The dog is connected to the kids, the kids are connected to the parent-teacher organization (PTO), the PTO is connected to the husband, the husband is connected to the mother-in-law, the mother-in-law is connected to the vacation, the vacation is connected to what we're going to eat Friday night, and Friday night is connected to how this meal is going to impact the grandkids, yet she doesn't even have any kids yet. Because, for a woman, everything is connected to everything, generally speaking.

Imagine opening your computer to every application on it and having it all open at the same time. That's the way a woman's brain typically works.

Now, how about the man's brain?

To draw an illustration of a man's brain, I would draw a bunch of separate boxes. Nothing is connected to anything. We have a work box. We have a family box. Inside that, we have a wife box and a box for each kid. We have a dog box, a TV box, a sports box, and many other boxes.

A man needs to process out of one box to get to the next box. But for a woman, everything's connected, so she can go from one conversation to the next and still be back over in the box of that first conversation. When a man and woman are communicating, the woman can go all over the place while the man is still locked into one of his boxes.

Men have two boxes that are bigger than any other box. One of those is completely empty. There's absolutely nothing in it. That's why, when our female friends, daughters, coworkers, or wives ask us, "What are you thinking?", we have the same response: "Nothing." They don't believe us. They don't believe you can actually think about nothing because, for them, every-thing is connected to everything.

We have another box that's bigger than everything else, and that's our sex box. So, our nothing box and our sex box are big-ger than any other box.

We must process out of our work box to get into our family box. And if we get into a TV box, we must process out of that TV we're watching to get back into the talking-to-our-kid box. But these two boxes, the empty box and the sex box, can be en-tered from any other box.

There's a piece of research that hasn't come out yet that I believe is true. I believe there's another box that no one's talked about yet, and it sits right between that empty box and the sex box. I call that the *clueless* box. This is our state of mind when we've done something but are totally clueless about what we've just done. The women in our lives exhibit changes in body lan-guage and get sad looks on their faces. But we have no idea what we've done. We're clueless. If you're married man or are working with women, the best thing you can do when that happens is to try to find out what you've done.

Wives, while you don't believe he doesn't know what he did, this is true, and the best thing you can do is to enlighten him. When I've done this to my wife in the past, I've said to her, "Honey, I know I just did something. I don't know what it is, and if you don't tell me what it is, I can almost guarantee you I'm going to do it again."

Men, if we can get out of our clueless box, we can have much better relationships with the women in our lives.

So, remember that (generally speaking), for women, everything's connected to everything. For men, nothing's connected to anything. If we can embrace this dynamic, we will improve our ability to communicate with those who think differently than we do—not only with our spouse and children but also with our coworkers. (I encourage you to do a little more research on this at LaughYourWay.com where you'll have a good laugh and learn a whole lot more about men's brains and women's brains.)

As my wife and daughters are bouncing all over the place in their conversations at dinner—e.g. John did this, and Susan did that, and then Mark did that, and Sally did this, and Joanne did this—I'll ask, "Who's John?"

My daughters will look at me and say, "What are you talking about, Dad?"

I'll say, "Well, you just said John did this."

"Oh, Dad, that was four conversations ago."

My box was way back over there, and they're all over the place. I have found great joy in being able to live with and laugh about these differences instead of getting irritated about them.

The same thing can happen at work. If we can laugh about what has happened, we won't get irritated. Our epinephrine (explained later in the chapter titled "Control Anger") won't kick in. But if we get irritated, our relationships will suddenly become more difficult.

Remember we're trying to become more relactional. We're trying to understand the opposite end of the relational-and-transactional continuum. We're trying to understand people who may think differently than we do. And, generally speaking, men and women think very differently.

Appreciate the differences.

One of my wife's love languages is *acts of service*, so I try to clean the kitchen frequently.[2] On one particular night, I was in my kitchen-cleaning box, cleaning the kitchen as I normally would. I emptied the dishwasher, scrubbed off the dishes that were in the sink, put the dishes in, opened the cabinet door, got the detergent out, poured it in the dishwasher, closed the door, pushed the button, put the detergent away, and closed the cabinet door. As I was completing this process, my middle daughter and my wife were behind me on the other side of the kitchen island having a slow, quiet chuckle. Slowly, the chuckle got louder and louder. Their laughing was contagious, so I started laughing, too, as I was going through my clean-the-kitchen box.

I then turned around and discovered they were laughing *at* me. I said, "Okay, what are you laughing at?"

My daughter said, "Dad, are you ever going to use that?"

I turned around, and right there in front of me on the kitchen counter was the dishwashing detergent. It was turned upside down, so I would use the last portion. I looked at her and asked, "How long has that been sitting there?"

She replied, "Three nights."

For three nights, I had almost knocked this thing over while cleaning the kitchen yet had totally missed it sitting there because I had been in my kitchen-cleaning box that is done the same way every time. So, as we laughed together, I told them, "Don't move the detergent out of my kitchen-cleaning box because I won't see it."

Years ago, I would have been offended and would have been hurt that they laughed at me. But now, equipped with an understanding of these things I've been sharing with you, we now can laugh at those situations, which improves our relationships. After all, don't we all want better relationships?

4

ACQUIRING THE TOOLS OF RELACTIONAL LEADERSHIP

IN THE REMAINDER OF THIS BOOK, you're going to learn practical ways to lead relactionally. Yes, you're going to have to check some old ways of thinking at the door. You'll see how to unlearn some bad habits. When you do this, you'll prepare yourself to embrace the tools, ingredients, and processes of relactional leadership that will help you and your organization to reach your potential.

But what does it take truly to learn new leadership habits?

Research shows that, if someone stands up and talks to us or at us lecture style, we can only remember approximately five percent of the content of that lecture 24 hours later. If we add some reading to that, the number goes to 10 percent. If we add some other audio-visual content, that number goes to 20 percent. If we do some demonstration, it jumps to 30 percent. If we have some discussion groups in which we talk with other people about what we are learning, it jumps to 50 percent. If we go out and practice what we learned, that number jumps to 75 percent. If we go and teach somebody else, that number jumps to 90 percent![3] It's astounding how much we can remember if we'll actually practice it and teach others while we're learning!

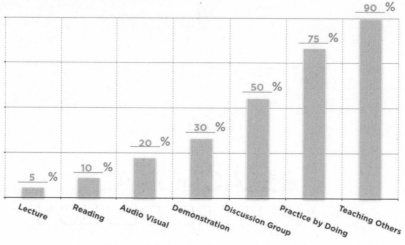

*Adapted from National Training Laboratories, Bethel, Maine

Think about it this way... *Tell me, and I'll forget. Teach me, and I'll remember. Involve me, and I'll understand. If I can understand it, I can own it. If I can own it, I can live it. If I can live it, I can teach, train, and equip others.*

This is why I encourage you to practice these tools as you are learning them. Teach others what you are learning because, now, you're involved. And because you're involved, your team will start getting involved. And once they get involved, they will learn and start living it.

Part 2

RELACTIONAL CONFLICT RESOLUTION

5

SOCIAL COVENANT

WHEN CONFLICT ENTERS any organization—that is, any time two or more people are in relationship—it not only makes it difficult relationally but can also cause the organization to underperform. A tool called the *social covenant* can help you to resolve any type of conflict you may encounter in your organization.

First, sit with a team member, your entire team, or your family, and ask this question: "When we're together, how do we want to treat one another?" Write down a list of words that describe how do you want to treat each other. You may write words or phrases like "respect," "honesty," "positively," "encourage one another," etc. Go ahead and start making a list here:

_____

_____

_____

_____

_____

After you agree with your team member(s) on how you're going to treat each other, ask this question: "How would we want to deal with it if one of us broke that agreement?" Or, "What process would we use to resolve the breaking of that agreement?" This section of the social covenant should clearly define action steps that would be followed if the social covenant is broken. Again, take a minute to write down what process you think would be best to implement.

_____

_____

_____

_____

_____

Remember that the process of dealing with conflict is not a process at all if it does not include some form of accountability. If you want to allow poor behavior and poor relationships into your organization, don't hold people accountable for their poor behavior. But if you want higher performance and healthier relationships, there must be accountability. It must be written into the agreement of how you are going to treat each other and how you're going to deal with it if that agreement is broken.

When the Social Covenant Has Been Broken

Here is the process I recommend that you put into your agreement in the event that someone breaks it.

1. Go one on one. If the one-on-one meeting resolves the conflict, the relationship has been restored. If this meeting does not result in a resolution, move to step two.
2. Take one or two others with you (that you mutually agree on), and try to have that meeting again.
3. Have a group of people that you trust listen to the conflict, and ask them to determine who is right in the conflict.

4. Whoever is deemed to be wrong, the accuser or
   the accused would then apologize or agree to
   leave the group.

This may seem like a tedious process. However, I have found that, if everyone agrees on how to treat each other, the process of resolution, and how to go one on one, a second meeting is seldom needed, and a third meeting is almost never needed.

When it comes to conflict, I have found that people generally fall into one (or more) of five categories:

1. **Sulkers** are those who just pout about what is going on but won't say what is wrong. They make it clear in their sulking that something is wrong but refuse to say what it is.
2. **Screamers** are the ones who get angry and yell at the other party (or parties) in the conflict. They become irrational, which can cause the other party (or parties) to become irrational.
3. **Pretenders** are the ones who act like everything is okay. They stuff their feelings down and just live with what is going on around them. Others may not be aware that they are feeling this way.
4. **Always-right** people have a high need to be right and approach conflict with the goal of winning and ensuring that the other party (or parties) loses. Such people are always trying to prove that they are right and that everyone else is wrong.
5. **Peacemakers** are the ones who remain logical and want to approach conflict in a way that restores relationship. They drive the other four groups crazy because they don't mind discussing conflict. They don't sulk over it, don't get angry about it, don't just let things go, and don't enable people to stay

in their muck. They have given up any need to be right because the relationship is far more important to them than being right.

The steps in dealing with conflict provide a process for people in any of these categories to move toward becoming peacemakers. When combined with "how" to approach someone, the process will go smoother and will give the parties a much higher chance to resolve the conflict and restore the relationship.

How to Approach Someone Who Has Broken the Social Covenant

When you approach someone who has broken the social covenant, it is critical that you approach the person in four ways.

First, go in *humility*. Be open to being wrong. In other words, go with the whole mindset, "I may be wrong." Even say to that person, "I may be wrong, but could I ask you a question? Could I share something with you?" Consider saying, "Maybe no one else feels this way or has ever shared it with you."

Second, go in *pre-forgiveness*. In other words, the goal of resolving conflict is to rebuild the relationship. We don't want to confront people because we're angry or hurt. We want to approach the person with an attitude of forgiveness. This doesn't mean you should tell the person that he or she is forgiven when you approach them; otherwise, this would nullify the statement, "I might be wrong."

Third, go in *love*. Care more about the other person than you do about how the other person feels about you. That is love. The goal is to remain in relationship with that person. If the person is hurting their relationships, it is important to love the person enough to tell him or her.

Fourth, go in *truth*. Don't deliver 80% of the truth because the other 20% is too difficult to bring up. That's not helping anyone. Give 100% of the truth. Sometimes, the facts and the truth can be different. For example, let's say you saw someone walk into another person's office and take some money out of that person's desk. The fact is that the person took the money. The truth could be that the other person left it there for that person to get. Go for the facts *and* the truth.

When you approach someone with humility, pre-forgiveness, love, and truth, over 95% of the time, the conflict will get resolved in one meeting.

The effectiveness of the social covenant rests completely on the extent to which everyone works toward its desired end. All members must be willing to be held accountable for themselves. Your team members must be willing to hold each other accountable as well. Keep in mind that, if you write a social covenant and don't implement it, you'll do far more damage than if you had never written it in the first place.

Now, let's move on to the next chapter where I'll share with you another relational leadership tool for conflict resolution.

6

SIX-STEP APOLOGY

ON ONE PARTICULAR NIGHT, we had many leaders at our house for dinner. People were in the living room, the dining room, and the family room. It was loud. People were talking, and we were gathering everybody in to begin eating dinner, which was setup as a buffet.

As people were coming in and talking, we were getting ready. Then, one of my teenage daughters went to the front of the line and grabbed a plate. When she did that, I looked at her and said, "Darling, you know our guests go first."

Right when I said that, it was one of those times when all the chatter had stopped, so it was dead quiet in the room, and all those guests heard me say that to my daughter. My daughter ran out of the room and upstairs to her bedroom.

I called our guests together and said, "You know... what I just did I've got to go fix. So you all go ahead and have dinner. I may be back tonight, and I may not be, but I've got to go take care of my daughter."

I went upstairs, and she was lying on her bed. I laid down next to her just for a moment. She rolled over and looked at me. I said, "You know, Sweetie, I just embarrassed you in front of all my friends. I just said something loud enough that everybody in the room heard it. And I was so wrong in doing that. And I'm so sorry. Will you forgive me?"

And she immediately said "yes" that she would forgive me.

I looked at her and said, "You know, Sweetie, you can hold me accountable to never do that to you again or even to your children one day when you have them. Because that's something I should never do as a father or later as a grandfather."

Then, I looked at her and asked, "Is there anything else you can think of that I might have done to you that would impact your life in the future? Because I don't want you to carry anything that I've done into your marriage or into your future. I always want you to know that you can talk to me about anything."

She looked at me and said, "Daddy, not anything I can think of right now."

I said, "Well, if you think of anything, you know you can always come and talk to me."

And then, I looked at her and said, "Okay, I'm going to go downstairs, and I'm going to apologize to all the people... all of our guests who are here. I can do that with you in front of them, or I can do it without you."

She said, "Dad, you don't have to do that."

I said, "I know that. But I don't want them to go home thinking that what I did tonight was appropriate in any way. Because I wouldn't want them to do that to their children. So would you like to come down now? Or do you want me to do it and you come down later?"

She said, "I think I'll come down later."

So I went back downstairs and asked everybody to stop eating just for a moment. I said to them, "You know, almost all of you heard me say to my daughter a while ago, 'Our guests go first.' And I want you to know that, for me to say that loud enough that you all heard it was wrong. And as I just told her upstairs, I say to you... I am really sorry that I did that in front of you. Because it's just wrong to do that to your children. I embarrassed her. And I want you all to know that, if I ever do that to you or to anybody around, you have permission to hold me accountable and tell me I did it."

And then, I said, "Is there anything else I've done to anybody else in this room I might need to apologize for?"

As I saw their response, I sat there with tears in my eyes because it's just that I didn't want them to go home thinking that was okay. I didn't want my daughter to go to bed hurt because her father had made that kind of mistake.

What is the right thing to do when your agreed-upon social covenant has been broken or when you have made a mistake that you are aware of? Answer: apologize.

So what is an appropriate apology? Is there a way to apologize that could lead to a change in behavior and save or grow relationships?

When apologizing, I recommend using a six-step apology. My team and I are often told that this tool has saved relationships that appeared to be beyond saving. We've been told it has saved unity in marriages, sports teams, companies, and many other types of organizations. Let's go through the process.

Step 1: State the offense.

State aloud to the other person what he or she believes you did to him or her. Say, "You are right. I did _____. I did that." If you have to qualify your apology by saying, "*If* I did _____", it's not a real apology.

Step 2: Acknowledge that you were wrong.

Use these three simple words: "I was wrong."

Step 3: Apologize.

It's very simple. Say, "I am sorry."

Now, if you were raised in a home where you were told you're a sorry little son of a gun, and that word has a different meaning for you, just say, "I apologize." Remember not to say, "I *want* to tell you that I am sorry" or that "I *want* to apologize."

These are not apologies. They are statements that you "want to" but are not going to.

Step 4: Ask for forgiveness.

Ask, "Will you forgive me?"

Only you know if you've used forgiveness as a way to control and manipulate others. If you have been doing this and have lost credibility as a result, ask the person, "When you can, will you forgive me?" Otherwise, ask for forgiveness on the spot.

It doesn't matter what the person's answer is. They don't have to say "yes" or "no," but it is important that you ask. Once you have asked, you have done your part. Regarding the relationship, the next step is now entirely up to the other person.

Step 5: Ask for accountability.

Tell the person who you hurt, "I give you permission to hold me accountable for not behaving this way anymore."

Remember that we're not making the other person accountable to hold us accountable. We're *giving permission* to the other person to hold us accountable. And those are very different.

When we say enough times, "I am wrong. I am sorry. Will you forgive me?", and we give permission for people to hold us accountable, our behavior will begin to change.

Step 6: Ask if there's anything else.

Ask the person, "Is there anything else I've done in our relationship that I need to apologize for?" When you ask that, you're going to surprise the other person.

Men, if you decide to do that with your wife, know that she remembers far more of the things you've done to her than you could imagine. You may not even remember what you did to her last week. So, if you take "step 6" in the six-step apology, be ready not to respond negatively. Just make a note of whatever she says.

Remember, if you go to someone else, go in love, humility, pre-forgiveness and total truth.

Write down a name or some names of people who you might owe an apology. Pick up the phone. Set up a meeting. Write down what you need to apologize for. Then, use the six-step apology, and see what happens in your relationship with that person.

Now, here's another example of what the six-step apology looks like in action.

To whom do you need to apologize?

One of the hardest things I've ever had to do is to share with my children something that I did to my wife many years ago.

My daughter called me from college and wanted to come to the Transformational Leadership Training in Orlando with two of her friends.

I said, "Hey, I really want you to come, but if you're going to come, will you come a couple of days early and just hang out with your old man?"

She said she'd love to do that.

The first morning she was there, we went for a walk. And on this walk, I said, "Darling, I have to tell you something, and I'm going to ask you to listen closely and hear me before you respond."

I went on to share with her about my infidelity... my adultery... my cheating on Sandra. I told her how wrong I was and made it abundantly clear to her that none of it had been her mother's fault.

After sharing with her how I had nearly destroyed our family, I looked at her and asked, "Is there any way you can ever forgive me for almost destroying our family and for what I did to your mother? Because it definitely has impacted you, too."

She looked up with a smile on her face and tears in her eyes and said, "Of course, Daddy. I forgive you."

When she said that, I looked at her and asked, "If you ever see me even glance too long at another woman who's not your mother, would you tell me that you noticed? Would you hold me accountable?"

I then asked her, "Is there anything else I've done in your life that would negatively impact anything that would happen to you. I don't want you to carry anything into your marriage that would result from something I have done."

I then explained to her, "If you or your future husband—whoever he may be—are ever tempted to do something like that, I want both of you to know that you have someone you can talk to before it goes too far."

As parents, spouses, friends, coaches, and bosses, we make mistakes. But do we know what to do to rebuild those relationships after we've made those mistakes? As I shared with you earlier, we've been told over and over that this six-step apology restores relationships. It restores them quickly. So, if there's someone you need to apologize to, go and do it.

7

How to Discipline

ONE OF THE THINGS WE DID in our sportswear company was to hire returning citizens, people who had been in prison and were in need of employment. We would hire and mentor them to help them reintegrate into society following their imprisonment.

One of our top returning citizens became our production manager. He was highly intelligent but got on the wrong path early in his life. When he came to work for us, he was then able to teach, train, and equip other returning citizens to help them move forward in life.

Another returning citizen had been on drugs and had been a thief before he came to work for us. He overcame his past to work his way into becoming assistant manual production supervisor. He supervised our workers who printed manually rather than with the automatic equipment we used to print most of our orders. When the production manager was out of town, the assistant would be in charge.

After our production manager had returned from a week of vacation one time, he came to me and said, "I have a problem."

"What's that?" I asked.

"There's something you gave me that was highly confidential. I had it in my desk drawer, and now, all the employees know about it. And the only person who had access to my desk drawer was the assistant."

"Have you talked to him?" I asked.

"Yeah, I went to him. He said he didn't do it. I'd like to go to him again with you."

So, I went with him, which wasn't good for the assistant given that I was his boss's boss. We went out on the floor, and I asked him, "Can we talk?"

"Yeah," he said.

"The manager tells me you took this piece of paper out of his drawer and shared it with the whole factory."

"That wasn't me," he pleaded.

I said, "Well, who else could have gotten into that desk in that office? You are the only two people who have a key to it."

"I don't know," he said. "Maybe the manager let it slip, but it wasn't me."

I told him, "You know there is no other way this got out because it happened when he was on vacation. You're the only other person who could've done this. So, are you sure you didn't do this?"

"I didn't," he said.

"I really believe you're lying to me right now, and you know we have a policy—in our policy manual that you signed when you came to work here—that if you steal, lie, or do sexual harassment, we don't have a choice. You won't get a second chance. If you don't come clean, you will leave me with no choice. But if you'll just come clean, we will work through this with you. You can stand in front of the employees, apologize for doing it, and this will all be done. It will be over like it never happened."

He said, "Ford, I would never do that to you after all the opportunity you've given to me. I wouldn't lie to you."

Saddened by his refusal to admit what he had done, I said, "Let me make it really clear. I love having you here. I love how far you've come. But you see that office door way up there?"

"Yeah."

"When I walk through that door, this opportunity is over. If I find out it was you and we can prove it, you know you won't have a job here. So, if you want to come clean, you have until I walk through that door."

He said, "I understand."

So, I went on that long walk back to my office because this was a rather large factory. Just about the time I stepped through and closed the door, I heard him yelling, "Ford! Ford! Ford!"

A few moments later, he came running into my office and said, "I'm sorry. I lied. I'm sorry. I'm sorry. I shouldn't have done it. I'll apologize to all the employees."

I said, "I'm sorry, too. No, you won't. I told you, once I walked through that door, this option would be over. So you have left me no choice."

He said, "But it was only three steps."

I said, "I know. But you know how I feel. You had that whole time to come clean, but you didn't. So, go get your stuff, clean your office, and go home."

He begged me not to fire him. I didn't fire him. This was his choice. He chose to leave when he refused to come clean before I walked back into my office.

When he walked out of my office, I sat there and cried. When someone like this gets his life turned around with that magnitude, the last thing you want to do is see him get hurt. So, he left, and I was heartbroken because we loved having him on our team. He was a great employee.

About three months later, I got a phone call from him. He asked me to have lunch with him.

"I'd love to go to lunch with you."

At lunch, he sat there with tears in his eyes and thanked me. He said, "Do you realize I had just started doing drugs again and was thinking about stealing again when that happened at the factory? If you hadn't told me to leave, I have no doubt my life would be right back where it was before, but that was a wakeup call. I just wanted to have lunch to say 'thank you' for standing your ground."

I believe people want that kind of leadership. I believe they want to be held accountable. I believe they want to know what the guidelines, policies, and expectations are—not in a constricting way, but they want to know what they are. When you have implemented clear guidelines, a social covenant, and clear discipline procedures, you'll eliminate the confusion.

In this chapter, you'll learn a model of discipline that works with employees and with children. However, I would caution you not to use this with your spouse. But it does work with people with whom you have influence (authority).

The Discipline Process

Discipline can be defined as "training to elicit a certain pattern or behavior." This isn't punishment. It's training.

How can we know who needs to be disciplined, when they need it, and how they need it?

The two main tools for discipline are *stories* and *questions*. If you have a story (an experience from your past) that would help the person who you are disciplining, share your story. This will lower the anxiety in the conversation. When you use questions to do discipline, it takes the pressure off you and puts it on the other person to make the right decision.

The Discipline Process

1: The Off-the-Record Meeting

Before you get to the two official meetings that will be documented, I would recommend that you have a one-on-one meeting that's only verbal. None of it would get written down. It would be somewhat of an off-the-record meeting. Often, that's all it will take to resolve relational or performance issues. I would consider this conversation part of teaching, training, and equipping. In the off-the-record meeting, use the same questions used in the recorded meetings discussed below. I have found that, when this process is done well, an official discipline meeting is rarely needed.

2: The First Recorded Meeting

If the off-the-record meeting does not get the point across, move into the first official recorded meeting.

As a reminder, discipline is done with stories and questions. Through the questions we ask, we are helping people to make sure they understand they've made a mistake. It is important that they understand they're either not performing at a high level or that their relationships or attitude aren't good.

Before you begin this meeting, write down some questions that address the problem. The key is to get the person being disciplined to acknowledge that he or she understands what the expectations are and that the expectations are not being met. Help the person to understand that his or her behavior is not appropriate and that it must change if that person wants to remain in your organization.

The following questions are not necessarily the exact questions that you would ask, but they provide a framework for your own set of questions that will address the specific problem you are trying to solve.

1) What are you doing that you are not supposed to be doing? Or, what are you not doing that you are supposed to be doing? Or, what behavior are you doing that is not acceptable to the organization?

2) What are you supposed to be doing? Or, what behavior is acceptable?

3) Are you actually doing what you are supposed to be doing? Or, are you actually behaving in the way that you are supposed to?

4) Do you understand the expectations and have we given you the tools you need to succeed? (*Note: When you ask this question, you may learn that the person truly did not understand the expectations.*) Or,

do you fully understand what behavior is acceptable and not acceptable?

5) Now, let's agree on how long it will take for you to do this. *(Agree on how long it will take and set a date and time for the follow-up meeting.)*

Make sure the person you're disciplining understands what you expect, whether relationally or regarding his or her attitude or work performance and that the expectations are not being met. Then, agree on when the changes will be made. Ensure that everything has been documented, that both of you sign it, and that the document goes in his or her employee file.

During this meeting, the person will most likely try to take you down a rabbit trail. **Don't go** down the rabbit trail with him or her. It will cost you a significant amount of time and will accomplish nothing. Keep asking the question you wrote down until the person answers it. Eventually, the person will get tired of you asking the same question and will finally answer it. Once the person answers it, move on to the next one until he or she has admitted to not meeting the expectations of performance or behavior.

Once the person has admitted the truth and affirms that he or she understands the expectations, ensure that the person has what is needed to succeed at meeting those expectations. At that point, move on to question number five and then set the follow-up meeting.

Let's assume you have a person who is chronically late to work. The person admits to having been late to work but now understands that he or she must arrive at work no later than 8:00 a.m. You then agree to assess whether the person's punctuality has improved within 30 days. The assessment meeting will be put on the calendar for 30 days from that agreement.

Then, be sure that the meeting takes place in 30 days.

3: The Second Recorded Meeting

If the person has been successful in doing what you've asked them to do, congratulate him or her in the follow-up meeting.

If you discover that the person has not done what was expected during the time allotted, continue in the process to the *second recorded meeting.*

As you can see below, the first three questions are identical to what was asked in the first recorded meeting. You wrote the answers down and put them in the person's file. Take them with you and ask them in exactly the same way. Again, don't let the person take you down a rabbit trail. Be sure that you stick with the question you asked until he or she answers it. Also, clarify how long the person will have to make the necessary changes.

1. What are you doing that you are not supposed to be doing? Or, what are you not doing that you are supposed to be doing? Or, what behavior are you doing that is not acceptable to the organization?
2. What are you supposed to be doing? Or, what behavior is acceptable?
3. Are you actually doing what you are supposed to be doing? Or, are you actually behaving in the way that you are supposed to?
4. Didn't we agree to… (See answer to #5 from the first recorded meeting.)
5. Let's agree on how long it will take for you to do it.
6. What will be the consequence of you not doing what you are supposed to do in the agreed-upon timeframe?

The big difference from the first recorded meeting is that there's now a sixth item; it's time to decide what the consequence will be if the person is unsuccessful.

You have heard it said that experience is the best teacher. I don't agree. *"It is the consequence of the experience that is the best teacher. No consequence; no teaching."*

If I am disciplining, the consequence following the second recorded meeting is probably going to be an agreement that this is not the place for that person to work. More than likely, there won't be a third recorded meeting with only me. The person's next meeting will be with the HR department to transition the person out of the organization. (I have tried three times at this point.)

Remember, at this point of the second recorded meeting, the decision is left up to the person being disciplined. You don't have to "fire" him or her. If the person meets the expectations in the time frame agreed on, he or she will still have a job. If not, the person has already agreed in the discipline process that the consequence is that he or she won't have a job in your organization. It's his or her choice, which takes the pressure off of you.

It is the same with kids. While you don't document the discipline as you would an employee, use the same story-and-question technique. If they do what they are supposed to do, the discipline does not take place. If they don't, the discipline does take place. If they know what is expected and what the result will be if they don't meet the expectations, and if you stick to it, you will be amazed how well children will perform and behave. While you would not send your child out of the home, he or she might be separated from the family or lose some benefit until his or her behavior changes. I believe change seldom occurs until the pain of staying the same exceeds the pain of change.

Parents and supervisors have told me repeatedly that this model removes a significant amount of stress from the discipline process. Why? You'll never have to fire anybody again. You will always make it the other person's choice. Your role as a leader is to make sure the options are clear.

Employee Steals from Company

Leaders at a company I formerly co-owned once asked me if I would be the speaker at their 30-year reunion. I was excited about the opportunity because I still had many friends who worked there. One of those employees had been there for almost the full 30 years.

As my wife was getting ready to go to the event with me, she asked, "Honey, are you ready to go?"

I said, "I am. But I'm confused."

"Why?" she asked.

I said, "Well, I got a phone call from the owner, and the company's leaders want to know if I'm okay if John [not his real name] comes. They don't want John to come. Why would they not want him to come? He was one of those first few people who helped us get the company off the ground, and they were bringing all those people back for the celebration."

She said, "Do you not remember what John did?"

I said, "What did he do?"

"He stole that money from us."

"Oh, I forgot all about that. I told him that I definitely wanted John and everyone else to be there. I haven't even thought about that in years."

So, I called back and said, "I had forgotten about that situation. If that's going to cause stress for somebody, I understand. But as far as I'm concerned, he is welcome to come."

The company leader said, "We want him to be there."

So, we went to the event, and I gave that talk.

After the event had concluded and we had reconnected with many old friends, nearly everyone had left. I then looked up and saw John and his wife standing across the room against the wall. Seeing that Sandra and I were preparing to leave, they walked over to me.

As they approached me, both John and his wife had tears in their eyes. We hugged each other, and he said to me, "You know… there's something I've never done. I've never apologized to you for the money I stole from you, and I've never thanked you for not sending me to jail."

Standing with him, his wife said, "Me, too. His life would be very different now."

We could have prosecuted him for his crime. On that day in my office, over 20 years prior, I said to him, "Normally, I would prosecute you because I think people are supposed to be held accountable for their actions. But I'm not going to do that. You're so talented and so young. I think you just made a mistake. But, let me make something really clear to you. If I ever hear that you've done anything close to this again, I will prosecute you for this because you know we can prove it."

I had no choice but to let him go because he signed the policy manual that stated there would be no second chance for that particular action.

Remembering that experience, John said, "Thank you for not prosecuting me."

His wife said, "Thank you. We have a wonderful marriage and have been successful since that time."

They both wept, as did I, as they expressed their gratitude.

As a leader, you can have a smart brain and a big heart and still be successful. That's relational leadership. Remember that discipline is training to elicit a certain pattern or behavior. Punishment is about you whereas discipline is about them.

8

CONFRONT SOCIAL ANXIETY

ALTHOUGH THERE WILL BE TIMES when discipline is necessary in relactional leadership, recognize that the vast majority of people genuinely want to do a good job. However, social anxiety makes it difficult for people to sustain high levels of performance.

Social anxiety happens when there are two things in play with us or the people around us: 1) there's a fear of failure plus 2) a motivation to be successful. When a fear of failure plus a motivation to succeed come together, this causes us to become anxious. This anxiety can cause us to underperform or to over-perform. If we put to rest those things that cause our team members to be anxious, they'll perform at a much better level.

When we're with our peers, the fear of failure and/or the motivation to succeed increase.

For example, if you have children, you're going to see your children come home many days full of social anxiety. On the first day of school, you're going to see them go to school with social anxiety, especially if they're entering a new grade at a new school. They have a fear of failure plus a motivation to succeed.

This also happens with salespeople, which can negatively affect the way they relate to customers. It can be a big cause of a new employee struggling to learn the new job. They could be spending much of their brain power that we want them to be using to learn their new job on something as simple as trying to remember everyone's name.

When this stress kicks in, it comes in two different forms. First, there's *distress*, which most of us know about. It's the kind of stress that causes us to underperform. It can cause us to shut down and perform at a lower level than we normally would.

The second form of stress is called *eustress*. Eustress is good stress. "Eu" is Greek for *good*. This good kind of stress can raise our levels of performance. But too much of it can cause us to overperform, which is just as bad as underperforming. For example, if the players on a basketball team have too much eustress, many of the shots they take will be long. If they have distress, many of their shots will be short.

The same thing can happen in a company. During the last week of the month in many production facilities, many companies will ship 80 percent of their shipping for the month. This isn't healthy for the workers. Then, in the first week of the next month, very little is accomplished. I call this the "end-of-the-month syndrome."

Both forms of stress, distress and eustress, can be equally hard on the body if we stay in either one of them for too long. Even though an appropriate level of eustress can be good, the key is not to stay in it too long.

If you have a team of people—whether they are your children, your employees, or the players on your sports team—one person's eustress could be another person's distress.

Try asking a group of people, "How many of you like to run?" Typically, a small percentage of the people will raise their hands. For that group of people, running is eustress. Those people experience something called "a runner's high." For the rest of the group, running creates distress.

The same thing happens when we're making decisions in any organization we're in. One decision will drive certain people's distress levels up while, at the same time, driving other people's eustress levels up. Later in this book, I'll show you more about why this is happening and how you can balance these two forms of stress in your organization.

Be aware that social anxiety is in play. But when it's in play, there is a way to take it out of play.

If you consistently use the tools, ingredients, and behaviors in this book, this will lower anxiety and keep stress in balance.

9

ELIMINATE GOSSIP

YOU'VE PROBABLY NOTICED that, when someone gets hurt or when conflict arises, people often tell other people about it. Unfortunately, the people they tell often aren't the ones who perpetrated the offense. This is an unhealthy and destructive practice called *gossip*. Gossip is when someone says something negative about someone to a person who is neither part of the problem nor the solution.

It has been said,

> Great people talk about vision and ideas. Average people talk about things. Small people talk about other people.

I add to that,

> Smaller people let them. Even smaller people join them. And even smaller people tell others.

Which of the categories above are you in most of the time? Do you ever fall into any of the "small people" categories? Which category are you in today, and which category do you want to be in going forward? The decision is up to you.

I get asked regularly how I respond to calls and emails so quickly when I get so many. I tell those people that one of the best time-management skills a leader can possess is not to get involved in gossip. It saves hours each week, enabling us to use our time more constructively.

It's extremely easy to get drawn into gossip. One of the things I do when people try to draw me into that kind of conversation is to ask them, "Am I part of the problem or part of the solution? Or, are you just gossiping about someone else?"

Nearly every time, the person will say, "I'm just seeking your counsel."

To which, I reply, "Well, I happen to have that person's number right here in my phone. Why don't we just call that person right now so you can share with him (or her) what you just shared with me?" Even if I don't have the other person's number in my phone, I do give the counsel to go talk to that person and not talk to others.

You would be amazed by how little actual gossip I hear now and how often I can be part of the solution if someone does come to me. They still come for counsel, but they know I will tell them to go talk to the other person after that counsel. That is being part of the solution.

Try this approach. You'll probably start to notice how many hours each week you would otherwise spend in those negative conversations about other people. We should care enough about others to talk to them directly about the ways in which they have offended us. And if we go in humility, pre-forgiveness, love, and truth, it will usually go well.

10

CONTROL ANGER

ON A PARTICULAR DAY MANY YEARS AGO, I got extremely angry while driving (aka. "road rage"). Sandra and I were dating at the time, and we were pulling out of the parking lot of a Skagg's Albertson store in Texas in my brand-new Ford Mustang. I had bought the car as a graduation present to myself. I was feeling pretty cool (aka. "self-centered").

As we were pulling out of this parking lot, another car pulled in front of me to try to beat me out of the parking lot. With massive road rage and knowing that I had the faster car, I zoomed around in front of them. As I went around them, I waved at them with both hands but only one finger on each hand as I drove with my knee.

Imagine how much anger I had triggered in that vehicle's occupants.

I exited the parking lot before they did and took a right turn onto the street. As I pulled up to the red light ready to go into the Texas A&M University campus, all the lights were red. As I looked in my rearview mirror, I saw two guys getting out of that car, both with a knife in one hand as they walked toward my car. Well, being a Texan, that wasn't a problem for me; you don't bring a knife to a gunfight. As I reached for my gun under my seat, Sandra reached over, grabbed my arm, and said, "No." Well, when she said that, I looked up, ran the red light, and drove away like a chicken.

If my wife hadn't been calm in that situation, there's a good chance I might be teaching transformational leadership in the

Texas penitentiary system today. How ridiculous would that have been to shoot somebody over who got out of the parking lot first? But that's what anger can cause us to do.

What pushes your buttons?

When people get angry, how do you normally respond to them? When someone comes at us with anger, most of us respond with more anger. Then, the other person responds with more anger. The cycle continues. Soon, there's a full-blown argument. How's that working for you?

There are three root causes of anger: fear, frustration, and pain (physical or emotional). When we become angry, an adrenaline called *epinephrine* (or *norepinephrine*) is released into our bodies, causing us to go into fight-or-flight mode. When we go into fight-or-flight mode, the rational part of our brain is inhibited, forcing us to rely on the emotional part of our brain. After expressing anger, have you ever thought or said, "I can't believe I said [or did] that! What was I thinking?" Well, now you know the truth; you *weren't*… "thinking."

When fear, frustration, or pain kicks in, what would happen if we could start changing the thought that occurs in those moments. For example, what if we immediately thought, *There's always one more thing about that person's life I know nothing about.* Or, what if we thought, *That person may have some hippocampus issues that are causing him (or her) to be angry. It may have nothing to do with what I just did.* Or, *Wow! Thank goodness this person cares enough about me to bring this issue to me so I am aware of it.*

If we can think like this when people get angry with us, we can prevent the epinephrine from releasing. However, if the epinephrine does release, the best thing we can do is to *remain silent*. Don't respond. Don't fight back. Don't take flight. Let the epinephrine run its course. Once the epinephrine runs its course, we can calmly deal with the anger we're both experiencing.

While sitting at a red light in Cincinnati, Ohio, I suddenly heard a loud honk from a vehicle that was approaching from the side. When I looked up, I saw that the honking was coming from a large conversion van that was swerving around me to avoid hitting me. As I had done in the previous story I shared above, the van's driver shot me the one-finger salute on the way by.

As I looked up, I realized I had rolled out into the intersection a little bit because I had been texting at the red light. I thought, *Wow! That man just saved our lives!*

Now, if my first thought had been, *That person has no right to shoot me the finger and blow his horn at me,* my epinephrine would have kicked in. Because my first thought was about how that man had just saved my life, I was able to process the situation more constructively.

So, I caught up with that van at a red light on the road. As I did, I was trying to signal to him to roll his window down. At first, he wouldn't. He finally rolled his window down. I looked at him and said, "Hey, back there, I was texting and didn't realize I had rolled out into the intersection. I was wrong, and I'm sorry. Will you forgive me for that? And thank you for being alert enough because you probably saved my life when you swerved around me."

And when I said that, tears welled up in his eyes. At that point, he probably wished he hadn't waved at me with one finger, but I was okay with it because I was the one who had caused him to have to swerve to avoid hitting me.

When we take this approach, our relationships will improve dramatically. If our relationships improve, we can shift the culture of any organization. And remember that an *organization* is when "two or more people are in relationship."

Take responsibility for your anger.

Imagine that someone allows his or her two-year-old child to grow up thinking she had the power to "make" him angry by regularly telling that child, "*You* made me so angry." As a teenager, that child would be continually doing the things that make him or her angry as a means to control that parent's life.

What happens if I look at a co-worker, friend, or my spouse and say, "*You* caused me to be angry"? Doesn't that sound silly? It's like saying, "*You* have complete control over my life." It doesn't make logical sense. However, this line of thinking may seem right to us when the epinephrine kicks in, keeping the rational part of our brain out of the situation.

Think new thoughts.

What "pushes your buttons"? What situations cause your epinephrine to release? Is it when your children don't do what you ask them to do? Is it when your employees underperform? Is it when your computer doesn't work well?

What specific thoughts come to mind that trigger the epinephrine to release in these sorts of situations?

Now, what are your new thoughts going to be that will help to prevent the epinephrine from releasing in response to these situations? Don't wait for these situations to occur before you decide what your new thoughts are going to be.

Stop right now and think of something that makes you angry. Then, write down the thought(s) you have in that situation that triggers the fear, frustration, or pain that causes the epinephrine to kick in.

Then, write down what a new thought can be or what the new thought is going to be the next time that happens. Start practicing that thought now so this will be the thought that takes place the next time that event happens. You will surprise yourself and those around you when you don't get angry next time. This will improve those relationships, make you the smartest person in the room, give you a powerful tool to use in other situations that would otherwise trigger your anger, and cause the productivity in your organization to increase.

Start now. Like building up a muscle, you'll be ready when the situation occurs. If you wait until it happens to come up with the new thought, it will be too late because the epinephrine will already have been released, the rational part of your brain will have been inhibited, and you won't be able to think clearly.

Use the six-step apology when you don't properly handle your anger.

In the past, my anger often surfaced while coaching sports. I've coached adults and children in many different sports, and I've gotten angry at nearly every level and in nearly every sport. I wouldn't ever yell at the kids, but I would "let the referees have it."

One night, we were having dinner with a group of couples with whom we met regularly for fellowship and accountability. I said to them, "I am really dealing with my anger issues and have made great progress with my family. But there's still one place where it comes out; that's coaching. I'm asking you all, including my wife… Would you hold me accountable to fix that, too?"

About six days later, we were having another elementary school basketball game. As we were warming up, a referee I knew walked in. He introduced me to his wife who also had on a referee uniform. He explained to me that this was her first day as a referee.

I thought, *You've got to be kidding. This is the first game when I'm going to work on my anger, and I have to deal with a brand-new referee?* During the game, the epinephrine was kicking in, but I was controlling it fairly well. She was just bad. She wasn't making one-sided bad calls. They were bad calls all the way around.

About three quarters into the game, I had reached my limit with her. Everybody was yelling and clapping for the kids. I looked at the male referee and said, "Come on, Man! Give her some help!" When I did that, the gym went silent. As I looked across the gym, I saw my wife watching the game. After asking her and others to hold me accountable for my anger just a few days prior, I had just yelled at the ref.

About an hour after we got home, my wife hugged me and said, "Honey, you may be the best coach with kids I have ever seen. But, you did yell at the ref. And when you did, the whole gym heard it. And you did ask us to hold you accountable."

It was time to offer a six-step apology to my wife. "Yes, Honey, you're right. I did that. I was wrong. I am sorry. Will you forgive me? And I continue to give you permission to hold me accountable. Is there anything else I did in that game that I need to apologize for?"

Here's the hard part. I then had to get back in the car, drive back to the gym, and wait until halftime of a game to apologize to those two referees. I went up to them and asked, "Can I talk to you?"

They said, "Yes."

I said, "You know… earlier today, I yelled this at you about your wife. I yelled, 'Come on, Man! Give her some help!' I was wrong for doing that, and I'm so sorry."

When I did that, they both started crying. And I thought to myself, it must have been much worse than I had thought. As they got their composure, I said, "I'm sorry to have caused that much pain. Will you forgive me?"

They looked back at me and said, "That's not why we're crying. You've been the kindest coach we've had all day. Everybody's been yelling at her."

Which leader has the most impact? The one who has been yelling at the ref nonstop or the one who messed up by yelling but then went back and apologized?

Which kind of leader do you want to be? It's your choice because you are in control of your own thoughts, feelings, and actions.

11

EMBRACING PERSONAL FEEDBACK

I ONCE HAD a dear friend who called me his "best friend," but he was very negative. I was trying to help him with that, but I wasn't getting very far.

As we were having coffee one morning, I looked at him square in the eye and said, "Do you believe I love you?"

"Absolutely. I believe that," he replied.

"So, can I give you some feedback?" I asked.

"Yes, you can."

I asked, "Is there anything I can't say?"

"Absolutely not. You can say whatever you want."

I said, "Brother, the truth is you are Eeyore. You are a downer. You empty my tank. You drain me when we're together. And the reason you drain me is you ask for counsel, but you don't use any of it. Your marriage isn't any better, your relationships aren't any better with your kids, and I can't do this anymore. So, I can't keep meeting and giving you counsel if you're not going to take the counsel and you're always going to drain my tank."

He immediately started crying like a little baby and just wept. He said, "No one has ever said that to me before."

I said, "I have news for you. If you'll go ask your wife and your children, they'll confirm it. And if they confirm it, the question is… are you willing to change?"

"If I am, can we keep meeting together?" he asked.

"Absolutely." I said. "But, if you don't, I'm done with giving you feedback and counsel. We can be great friends, but don't ask for counsel anymore."

The very next meeting we had, the first thing he did was to start asking me about my wife, my children, and our company. He wanted to know how we were doing. He had made significant changes to his attitude. Since then, I have received thanks from his wife, his children, and his friends.

Even through negative feedback—when it is done with humility, love, truth, and forgiveness—we can make a positive impact on peoples' lives. All personal feedback is relevant.

All feedback is relevant.

Research shows that, once our self-identities have become set, they're extremely difficult to change. Later, if we get feedback that is already consistent with our identity, it goes right in and builds on top of what we already believe about ourselves. And if we get feedback that we don't believe, we tend to reject it.

While all personal feedback is not true, I believe all personal feedback is relevant. It's important to be open to feedback you may not believe to be true *just in case* it is true. This applies to positive and negative feedback.

Also, personal feedback is relevant to your relationship with the person giving it. The feedback given could determine whether you want to stay in that relationship with that person.

It's also relevant to your own character. If someone was driving down the road and shouted out something offensive at you, your response to that feedback would say something about your character. It will also make a profound impression on your children or others that might see your response.

As leaders, our response to personal feedback could determine the level of influence that we might have with someone.

Interpreting Feedback Constructively

Sometimes, the hardest feedback to receive could be that which is shared between a husband and wife. During the time when I was struggling in our marriage, we went to a marriage conference. I wanted help, and I didn't know where else to go.

At this conference, they told us to tell our spouse one thing we wanted them to change about themselves. My lovely bride looked at me and said, "I want you to lose some weight." I had put on about 60 pounds during that season of frequent traveling. Because of the poor condition of my self-identity at the time, what I heard was, "You're fat and ugly, and I don't want to be with you."

But what she really meant was, "I love you, I want you to be healthy, and I don't want you to die at an early age."

Why did I interpret what she said so negatively? As a child, I was a little fat boy. I had been sexually abused. How did I cope with that abuse? I ate. Later, I lost the weight but then put it back on due to the frequent travel and stress. When she said, "I want you to lose some weight," I heard something very different than what she had actually said.

If our self-identities are messed up, we may reject essential feedback, get angry, and let the epinephrine kick in because we heard something very different than what the other person said.

But that feedback was highly relevant even though my epinephrine went up and I responded in a negative way. But now, she can give me that feedback because I know she's doing it because she cares about me.

We might never hear what we need to hear if we aren't willing to offer and receive personal feedback.

T.F.A.

In my company and in many companies with whom I work, we have a little code we use if we see someone who might be behaving in a way we know they don't want to behave. We'll just tap three times on the table or on the person's shoulder. The taps simply communicate to the person,

The way you're behaving right now is not consistent with who you say you want to be. So, right now, change the *thought*, change the *feeling*, and change the *action*.

In short, the taps mean "T.F.A.," which stands for "thought, feeling, action." Many of us have cultivated such a relationship that we can just say aloud, "T.F.A.," which prompts us to pause, change the thought, change the feeling, and change the action—which improves and grows relationships.

Affirm before correcting.

When we give negative feedback in the right way, it will have been preceded by many affirmations. Then, when it's time for some correction, the recipient will be more open to it. If we do it really well, even the correction can feel like an affirmation because they're encouraged to be the best version of themselves. And I believe that's what we are trying to do as leaders. We have the opportunity to lead people with whom we have influence to reach levels of potential they never thought possible.

Part 3

RELACTIONAL COMMUNICATION

12

How We Communicate

SOME RESEARCH SHOWS that everything we communicate falls into three major categories. Approximately 55% of what we communicate happens through our *body language*, 38% happens through our *tone of voice*, and only 7% of what we communicate is through our actual *words*. In other words, if I'm saying one thing but my body language and tone of voice are inconsistent with what I'm saying, I have little to no credibility. In other words, the words lose all their credibility if the body language and tone of voice don't line up.

Here's an example: "Love ya!" When someone says that, does it really feel like the person is saying, "I love you" when his or her tone of voice and body language seem so aloof?

When our body language, tone of voice, and words are all lined up, even if it's negative, we have credibility. When it's positive, we have even more credibility.

When I was in my early 30s, we had grown a company to a fairly large size, and a group of venture capitalists came to me and said, "We want to take a look at buying your company." They ended up buying a large part of it. I then joined a group of companies that were going to buy other companies like ours and put them all together to form a bigger company. As we did this, the venture capitalists had the chairman-of-the-board seat in our company, and each of us remained presidents of our own individual companies. We would meet as a board on a fairly regular basis and talk about business.

During that time, I was the youngest guy in the room, and I was pretty cocky and arrogant—okay, I was quite a bit more than a little cocky and arrogant. Our company continued to be profitable month after month while some of theirs were up and down, which is normal for most businesses. So, as they would say things I thought were dumb, I would unknowingly and rudely express my distaste for their ideas with my facial expressions.

One day, I got a phone call from one of the men who was on that team. He said, "Can I come see you?" I agreed, so he came to my office and said, "Can I share something with you?"

I said, "Yes."

He said, "Did you know that, in our meetings, when we say something you don't think is very intelligent, you do things like roll your eyes, breathe heavily, and cross your arms? Your body language... it just kills us. We've had a meeting without you, and we know that we need an operational CEO... not just a chairman who comes to our meetings but someone who's in the company. We've all talked about it. You're the guy. The problem is we can't work for you. It's because of your body language and facial expressions that come across as arrogant, and we feel stupid when you do it... and we can't handle that."

I was in my mid-30s and started crying. It broke my heart. I had no idea I had been doing that, which meant I probably had been doing it everywhere.

A few weeks later, we had another board meeting. I hadn't realized before that day, but in every meeting, the chairman would sit in the same chair. About an hour into the board meeting, the chairman said, "Hey, Guys, can we all take a break?" We agreed. He then said, "Ford, would you come with me?"

We went into an office and closed the door behind us. He said, "Hey, are you feeling okay today?"

I said, "Actually, I'm feeling better today than at any previous board meeting. Why do you ask?"

He said, "I make 95% of my decisions based on your facial expressions. And, today, you're not telling me anything."

I said to him, "You'll never be able to hear anything from me again based on that."

A few months after that, the team came to me and asked me if I would be the CEO of the whole company. For a period prior to that, the company's profitability had stagnated. I had been blaming all of them because their companies weren't doing as well as mine.

Once I fixed my body language, facial expressions, and tone, the team worked together, and we grew the company at a fast rate. What had been holding us back previously? Could it be possible that something as minor as body language (facial expressions) could hinder a company, church, school, sports team, or family from reaching their full potential?

Be aware of whether your words are lining up with your body language and tone of voice. Otherwise, you're at risk for doing great damage to your relationships and your organization's productivity.

13

FIRST IMPRESSIONS

LET ME TELL YOU ABOUT A BAD FIRST IMPRESSION I made. Soon after I first met Sandra at Texas A&M University, we were at a dance and ended up dancing for a while. For the rest of that week, we laughed and joked around together, getting to know each other better. I'm a bit of a jokester, probably even more so then than now.

Her birthday was the following week, and on her birthday, I decided to go by her dorm room and tell her happy birthday. After I knocked and she had opened the door, I said, "Hey, Sandra, I know today is your birthday, so I came by to say 'happy birthday.' And for your birthday, I'm going to let you kiss me on my cheek."

Playing along, she said, "Ooh!" And she gave me that kiss. Then, she opened the door all the way and said, "Hey, while you're here, let me introduce you to my mother and my older sister."

Now, can you imagine the first impression I had made on my future wife's mother and older sister? With her older sister, it might not have taken 20 additional encounters to undo that; it might have taken 20 years (joking here).

The Value of a Good First Impression

Research shows that it takes 30 seconds or less to make a good first impression. Some studies have shown that it may only take a split second.

Research has also shown that it takes approximately 20 additional encounters to overcome a bad first impression. Now, if we make a bad first impression, what is the likelihood that we're going to have 20 additional encounters with that person? If we go to church with, go to school with, are on a sports team with, or work with the person, we might have those opportunities. But outside of that, we probably won't have an opportunity for 20 additional encounters. But if we did, we wouldn't be able to use these additional encounters effectively if we didn't even realize we had made a bad first impression.

If we were aware that we had made a bad first impression, what tool could we use to overcome it? We could use that six-step apology if we were at fault. We could just admit that we did it, say we were wrong, apologize, ask for forgiveness, and give him or her permission to hold us accountable for not coming across that way anymore. Then, we can ask, "Is there anything else I have done that I need to apologize for?"

Is it possible we can make a bad first impression and not have done anything wrong?

Have you ever met somebody and thought, *I don't really like that person, but I can't quite put my finger on why.* Unbeknownst to you, there may be something in your hippocampus that prevents you from liking that person. It could be because of something as simple as a shirt, a particular type of smile, or a word the person said.

In our organizations, good first impressions are critical. If we make a bad first impression on a customer or a person in another type of relationship, the person probably will not come back a second time. If you went to a restaurant and got a bad meal and bad service, you're probably not going to return there 20 more times to allow that restaurant the opportunity to revise your perception of their food and service.

We all must be careful about those first impressions and what we are communicating to people when we interact with them the first time. Be aware of how you are coming across.

14

AFFIRMATIONS

TO *AFFIRM* SOMEONE is to say something positive about someone directly to him or her. It is about saying something positive to the person about who he or she is. Or, it could be thanking someone for something he or she has done for you. Think of someone who has done something for you. Maybe you think the person knows you appreciate the favor, but maybe you've never actually told him or her. Consider affirming that person directly, and see what happens. Let's explore how to do that.

Remove insincere phrases.

First, remove phrases in your affirmation like "I would like to" or "I want to." Have you ever watched those award shows on television when the people go up, get their award, and say, "*I would like to* thank my mom and dad. *I want to* thank my spouse. *I would like to* affirm the director." But if you pay close attention, they never actually thanked or affirmed those people.

When you remove those kinds of phrases, your affirmations will be much more genuine and sincere.

Make eye contact.

When you're affirming someone, be sure to look the person in the eye to communicate sincerity.

Yes, in some cultures, making direct eye contact is disrespectful. So, if you're living in or working in a culture like that, this may not be appropriate. In other cultures, making eye contact is customary. So, make the decision based on the cultural context.

Make it about the other person. (Don't use flattery.)

If you make it about you, it's not an affirmation; it's flattery. If you're doing it to get something out of someone, that's flattery. If you do it to make yourself look good, that's flattery. An affirmation is completely about the other person while flattery is completely about you.

Be honest.

Don't tell somebody something that's not true. The person might end up singing on a TV show somewhere, getting made fun of because you told the person he or she was good at singing. Don't tell a child, for example, that he can be the superstar of the sports team if he or she is exceptionally slow and isn't very athletic.

Be sure that the affirmation is truthful and not a lie just to make someone feel good.

Affirm the person *directly*.

Talk *to* the person; don't just talk *about* the person. He or she is right there in the room with you.

Now, there's nothing wrong with sitting in a room and talking about how great someone else in the room is, but that's not an affirmation. An affirmation happens when you turn toward the person, look at them in the eye, and talk to the person about himself or herself.

When and Who to Affirm

An affirmation could be a *thank you*. "You did this for me, and I really appreciate it. Thank you so much for that." It could be about who they are. It could be something that's so obvious but that no one tells them. It may be obvious to everyone else but not to that person.

Before the day is over, either pick up the phone and affirm someone over the phone (which means you can't look at them in the eye), or meet with the person to affirm him or her face to face. Thank the person for something he or she did for you, or share something positive about who the person is.

Being an affirming person and building an affirming culture in your organization will literally shift your organization into a whole new place and onto a whole new level. If done well and if they become a part of a culture, affirmations can improve productivity while helping to improve people's self-identities and remove lies that might be stored in their hippocampuses.

When you make that phone call or meet with that person face-to-face, don't forget that an affirmation is about the other person while flattery is about you.

15

S.L.O.W.E.R. LISTENING MODEL

RELACTIONAL LEADERS ARE GOOD LISTENERS. What does good listening look like? I call it the *S.L.O.W.E.R. listening model.* This simply means slow down and listen. Let's break down this acronym.

S = *Square up* and be *silent.*

To be a good listener, square up to the person you're talking to, face him or her, be silent, and listen to what the person has to say. Silence is one of the hardest tools for a leader, especially for one who likes to process out loud as I do. Let the room get uncomfortable. Allow those who process internally to have the time to process before moving on to the next subject. You might be amazed by some of the great ideas that the internal processors will come up with if given the time to process while you go silent.

L = *Lean into* the conversation.

Lean in and listen. Show interest.

As you're leaning into conversations with people, be aware of the person's personal space. Most people get uncomfortable when someone is standing too close to them as they are talking. If you are like me and don't really have a "personal space", be very careful not to step into someone else's. You can know by reading the person's body language and facial expressions. If they back away a bit, you will know that you have stepped into the person's space. If you do, gently and simply back out of it.

O = Maintain an *open* posture.

Don't be closed off when you're listening. If your body language is closed off, people won't be sure if you're listening or not. Remember that 55% of our communication occurs through our body language—even if we are not talking.

Also, when you're talking to someone, ask *open*-ended questions. Give the person an opportunity to talk more. Don't just ask yes-or-no questions. Open it up for the person to talk so you can listen.

Especially with children, consider asking open-ended questions instead of simply, "What did you do today?" Most often, the response will be, "Nothing."

W = Be *willing* to be engaged.

You may see the need to turn around from your computer to put down your cellphone in order to listen. Demonstrate willingness to be engaged in the whole conversation and with your whole body.

E = Make *eye contact*.

Look at the person who is talking to you. Listen with your ears as well as your eyes.

Yes, eye contact is not appropriate in some cultures, so please apply this principle judiciously if you are in one of those cultures.

R = Relax, respond, and repeat.

When you're listening, relax, respond, and maybe even *repeat* back (if necessary) what the person said to ensure that full communication took place.

If you'll learn to apply this S.L.O.W.E.R. listening model, the people you're with—whether at home, in your workplace, or in whatever sphere you're in—will feel more confident that you care about them because you'll be more engaged with what they are saying.

Remember that 55% of communication is through body language. This not only applies to talking but also to listening.

16

EMAIL ETIQUETTE

A SIGNIFICANT PORTION OF OUR COMMUNICATION happens through email. I couldn't imagine conducting business within an organization without it anymore. A key part of my growth as a transformational leader was learning how to communicate properly and effectively through email. (I still mess this one up on occasion, so be patient with yourself.)

Chances are, you've misinterpreted an email or had one of your emails misinterpreted at some point in your life. Email can quickly trigger unnecessary conflict. Here are a few tips to use email as an effective communication tool.

1: Don't read energy or emotion into emails.

All you have in an email are words, which only account for 7% of communication. The other 93% of communication happens through body language and tone of voice, which cannot be seen or heard through text alone. As we keep this in mind, it will be easier to restrain ourselves from responding back with negative energy or emotion.

2: Use a greeting in your emails.

Start off with something as simple as the person's name or a simple greeting (e.g. "I hope you are having a nice day.). This will help to prevent the person from reading negative emotion or energy into your email.

3: Use the communication channel on which you want the person to respond.

If you want the person to call you on the phone, call him or her on the phone. If you want the person to respond by text, send a text. Don't text someone and say, "Call me." Don't email someone and say, "Text me." Don't email someone and say, "Call me." That's not fair. That's putting your responsibility onto someone else. How would you like to get 20 emails or 20 texts from 20 different people in one day saying, "Call me when you get a chance"? If text or email is the preferred form of communication, a simple voicemail after the text, reminding the person that you left the text or email asking them to call is an easy solution.

4: Be careful about using bold or all caps.

Bold or all caps can easily communicate to someone that you are yelling at him or her. When using bold or all caps, be careful to emphasize that you are using them only to point out a section or a thought to make it easier for the reader to find—not as a means to imply yelling.

5: Use a clear subject line.

A good subject line will help you to stay in communication about an issue as you're working through it.

6: If addressing several topics, use bullet points or numbering.

Don't write the email like it's a letter. Don't use paragraphs that bury a question or a point in the middle of it; otherwise, it will be easy for the reader to miss it. But if it's a bullet point or a number, there is a much better chance that they'll get the point.

Also, if you want to reply down in the body of an email, use all caps, a different font or color. If someone sends a list of bullet points or questions, just say at the top, "I'm going to answer below in a different font and in all caps [or in a different color] to make it easier to find my responses."

7: Keep conversations intact.

When you're going back and forth in emails, be sure that the original email is in there and that it remains in there until all the communication related to that issue is finished. The previous emails should remain in the correspondence for reference. That way, you'll help to prevent the person from responding to the wrong email, especially if you have multiple email communications going with the same person.

8: Limit sending carbon copy (Cc) or blind carbon copy (Bcc) emails.

I strongly encourage you to be very careful about how you use the carbon copy (Cc) or blind carbon copy (Bcc) features. You can use them for FYIs if you want someone to get some information. And make it clear as to whether you want people to "reply all" so they don't do that unless necessary. That way, your people won't get dozens of unwanted or unneeded emails in their inboxes. Bcc is also good to use as a way of preventing people from sending an email via "reply all."

Don't use Bcc to give information to someone that you don't want others to know you sent to him or her. This will often end up getting out and causing conflict and a significant waste of time. It sounds so simple, but so many do it.

9: Don't resolve conflict through email.

If there's a conflict going on, pick up the phone or speak with the person face to face. When we try to solve conflict through email (or texting), we're only prolonging and often escalating the conflict. And remember that the recipient of the message is only getting 7% of the message, which can elongate and escalate the conflict.

10: Avoid using words in the wrong context.

One word that is often misused in email as well as verbal communication is the word *need*. For example, "You *need* to do this" or "I *need* you to do this." Save the word *need* for something you really do need.

Also, avoid misusing or overusing words like *should* or *must* in statements like, "You *should* (or you *must*) do this." *Should* is a shame word, and *must* can be controlling.

Be careful about using the word *but*. Often, people will give an affirmation and then say, "But…" That's called transitional praise and will cause the person to forget how you affirmed him or her and only focus on what comes after the "but."

Be careful about using words like *always* and *never*. "You *always* do this." "You *never* do that." It's usually not true.

11: Ban cussing.

I get a lot of pushback on this one, but I am okay with that. Are you impressed when people cuss at you or in front of you? If not, then you can be pretty sure that they are not impressed with you when you do it. I suggest that you cut out the cussing in your organization and in your personal life. Those four-letter words aren't helping you. They don't add productivity. As a matter of fact, they can lower productivity.

17

HOW TO HANDLE UPSET PEOPLE

MANY YEARS AGO, a customer came into our place of business and had a photograph she wanted us to print on a t-shirt. It's hard to imagine given today's technology, but printing a photo on a t-shirt wasn't done much back then. I told her it wasn't possible to do that.

She said, "I was wondering about those pictures I see on the wall."

What she saw were pictures of animals that looked like photographs that were hand done. But we did those for large retailers who placed large purchase orders for shirts, which justified the time required to do that intricate, time-consuming artwork. I explained this to her. I'm not sure she believed me, but it was the truth.

As the customer service representative and I were explaining this to her, our art director walked by. He looked up and said, "Can I have a shot at that?"

I said, "You know we can't put a picture on a t-shirt."

"Maybe we can now. Our new Apple just came in," he said.

"What's an Apple?" I asked.

"You approved us buying it." He then explained to me that it was our new computer system.

I looked back at our customer and said, "Do you want us to try?"

So, we produced the sample with our new Apple computer and were so excited. We knew this would put us on the map in the screen-printing industry.

The customer came in, looked at it, and was extremely happy. She gave us a nice-sized order of those shirts to sell in her retail store. So, we made the shirts, and she returned a few days later to pick them up.

When she returned, I happened to be downstairs standing in the doorway, watching her with the customer service rep as she picked them up. As they were talking, I could see that she was happy. She wrote the check, and someone went to get the shirts to load them into her car.

As she was writing the check, someone came to talk to me, so I turned away and started taking someone on a tour of our facility. Suddenly, I heard her yelling at our customer service rep. I had no idea what had happened, but she was angry and screaming. I watched our customer service rep do what she was supposed to do, just sitting there calmly and listening. But this lady was not stopping, and she started cussing at our customer service rep.

Well, that was enough for me. I walked over and said, "Ma'am, can I help you?"

She picked up the shirt and she said, "Look at this!"

I looked at them and couldn't see anything wrong with them. She reached in her purse and pulled out a magnifying glass to show me what we refer to in the t-shirt industry as a "pinhole." That's when a little bit of stray ink comes through the screen onto the shirt. And if you see one, you can spray it out with a special spray, and everything is fine. But if you can't see it with the naked eye, you don't even know it's there. But with this magnifying glass, you could see this little pinhole way down below the logo.

I said, "Yes, Ma'am. I see exactly what you're talking about."

I looked at the customer service rep and said, "I noticed she gave you a check."

She said, "She did."

"Could I have her check?" I said.

She handed the check to me. I got some assistance from another employee, and we loaded all the shirts into the customer's car. Then, I looked at her and handed her the check.

I said, "You know, Ma'am. I understand that there's a little pinhole in that shirt that you can't see it with the naked eye. It's not going to impact the sales of shirt. However, you can have the shirts, and here's your money back. But let me make something really clear to you. No one cusses at my employees. Don't you ever come back to my company again unless you're willing to apologize to her for the way you treated her."

About a week later, one of my employees called me in my office and said, "Ford, Mrs. B is on the phone." (At this point, she had a nickname in our company.) I picked up the phone and said, "Hey, Mrs. B. What's up?" (I didn't actually call her "Mrs. B.", but I sure thought about it.)

"Best-selling shirt I've ever had!"

I said, "I'm really happy for you."

"I really need you to make some more," she said.

"Yes, Ma'am."

She explained, "Well, your staff downstairs told me they can't take my order."

"That's not true," I said. "We'd be happy to make them for you."

"You would?" she asked.

"Yes, Ma'am. All you have to do is come down and apologize to that lady you cussed at."

"You can't make me do that."

"You're absolutely right. I cannot make you do that."

Perplexed, she asked, "But you'll make my shirts?"

"Yes, Ma'am. I'm happy to make your shirts. All you have to do is come down and apologize."

"You can't make me apologize to that girl."

"No, Ma'am. I cannot make you apologize."

"I really need these shirts," she declared with frustration in her voice.

"Happy to make them for you," I said. "All you have to do is come apologize."

I could sense she was getting angrier and angrier. I said, "Ma'am, let me help you here. We have five competitors in town. Let me give you their names and phone numbers, and you can call them."

"I've already called them. They can't make this."

Yes, I'm aware of that, I thought to myself. "But there are national competitors. Maybe they can," I said.

"I can't find anybody who can print a picture on a t-shirt."

"Yes, Ma'am," I said. "I tried to explain that to you."

"I really need these shirts."

"Would love to make them for you."

"You would?"

"Yeah, all you have to do is come apologize to that lady."

Boom! She slammed the phone down in my ear. So I called downstairs and said, "Hey, she hung up on me."

About 30 minutes later, I get another call. "Hey, Ford... Mrs. B is down here."

I went downstairs, and there she was. I walked up to her and said, "Hey, Mrs. B. It's good to see you."

"Is there any way I can get you to make these shirts?" she pleaded once again.

"Yes, Ma'am. She's sitting right over there."

"You would make me do that?" she asked.

"No, Ma'am... I would not make you do that. This is totally your choice."

"I'll do it," she said.

"Hang on just a minute," I said.

"What?"

"That day you cursed at her, our whole front office heard it. They're all going to hear you apologize."

"You would make me do that?"

"No, Ma'am... This is totally your choice. If you apologize, we'll make the shirts. If you don't, we won't."

"I'll do it."

We gathered everybody around, and she apologized.

I then called the production manager.

He came up and said, "What's going on?"

I said, "Mrs. B said this is one of the best-selling shirts she's ever had. She's out of shirts and wants to know when we can make some more."

He said, "Well, let me check the production schedule... Ford, will you come with me?" As we were walking away and he was looking at the production schedule, he said to me, "I thought we weren't going to do business with her anymore."

"Oh, Man!" I said. "I should have brought the whole factory up! No, I'm kidding. She apologized."

"She did?"

"Yeah, in front of the whole staff."

He walked back over to Mrs. B and said, "Ma'am, let me go check deeper into the schedule. Right now, we're about two weeks out, and I understand that you're out of shirts, so let me check."

He came back to her and said, "If I could have these shirts finished by 5 p.m. today by moving some things around, would you be able to pick them up today?"

A tear came into her eye. She looked at him and said, "You would do that for me?"

"Yes, Ma'am. You're one of our best customers."

Seven-Step Process for Handling an Upset Person

What's the best way to handle an upset person?

1: Remain silent.

As soon as a person has finished expressing his or her anger toward you, be silent and don't respond. Why? Because the person's epinephrine has not run its course. He or she probably isn't finished unloading on you.

2: Remain silent.

When the person comes at you again, remain silent. Why? That person is probably going to come at you again because his or her epinephrine is still releasing.

3: Remain silent.

Again, remain silent.

People often ask me, "Why is it that you tell us to remain silent for so long, and how do we know when not to remain silent?" The way you'll know is by the person's *intensity* level and *duration* of the anger. The intensity and duration of the person's anger will go down as the epinephrine runs its course. As you see the intensity go down and the duration getting shorter, you'll know it's time to respond.

If you give a response too soon, the person will probably cut you off. I'm sure you've seen this before. You probably have even done it. The person cuts you off, starts going again, and won't even remember what you said because the rational part of his or her brain is inhibited in the moment. So, the best way to save time and the relationship is to remain silent until the angry person is not angry anymore.

4: Thank the person for the feedback.

Once we notice that the person's intensity level has subsided, I recommend that your first response be to thank the person for his or her feedback. Say to the person, "It's this kind of feedback that helps our organization to improve." Or, you might say, "It's this kind of feedback that helps me to improve as a leader."

Then, quickly add, "May I repeat that back to you to be sure I understand?"

5: Repeat back to be sure you fully understand what the person is saying.

When you do this, there is a good chance the person will say, "I didn't say that," even though you know he or she did. Don't get mad. Don't get offended. Don't assume the person is lying. He or she probably doesn't remember saying it because the rational part of that person's brain isn't functioning at its full capacity. The person isn't necessarily lying.

This is one reason why many large companies record customer service interactions. Neither the customer nor the agent can get away with saying, "I didn't say that." The recording will verify exactly what was said.

When you repeat back what you heard the person say and the person says, "I didn't say that," just ask again. "Will you say that again to be sure I understand?"

6: Make a commitment and follow up.

Once you have a full understanding of what was said, 1) make a commitment to action and 2) follow up on that commitment. What's the difference between these two steps?

First, you must make a commitment to act on what the person has shared with you. For example, let's say a customer is angry toward one of your employees, but the employee the customer is upset with isn't in the office. My commitment to the customer would be this: "I'll call you back in 24 hours. That person will be back in tomorrow."

Second, you must follow up on that commitment to action. Maybe the employee got stuck in a place without cellphone coverage and can't get back to town. Well, within 24 hours, you still must call the customer and fulfill the commitment you made.

7: Make a commitment and follow up on the problem once you have all the details.

Once you get all the information you need to make a decision, you must make a commitment to act in order to make it right. If your organization was wrong, the best thing you can do is to apologize. After you have spoken with your employee, I suggest that the person who made the mistake should do the six-step apology. It is a great training moment for the person, and you are also making sure that the employee isn't being thrown under the bus with the customer by you making the apology.

Next, tell the customer how you have improved, that your organization was wrong in what you did, and that you are sorry. Then, ask for forgiveness. Explain that the person is a valuable customer and that you want that person to hold your organization accountable to always do what you say you'll do. Then, ask if there is anything else your organization has ever done for which you need to apologize.

As I have continually told those who work with me in the organizations I've owned or consulted with, you are going to make mistakes. I am going to make mistakes, too. If you're going to make a mistake, please don't make one so big that it puts our organization out of business.

However, if you make a mistake with a customer, this process will enable you to win a customer for life. Not only does this process work with an upset customer, it also works with an upset child, spouse, employee, friend, or boss. Remain silent. Remain silent. Remain silent. Let the person's epinephrine run its course. Thank the person for his or her feedback. Repeat back to the person what he or she said.

Then, make a commitment to find a solution. If the customer, you, or your employee was in the wrong, explain the wrongdoing and move forward with the solution. Then, follow up to make sure the solution gets implemented.

The customer is *not* always right but is always the customer.

If you or your organization were not in the wrong, the solution may not necessarily be that you need to apologize.

Statements like "the customer is always right" and "the customer comes first" have been common adages in the business world. Yet, those statements are not true. To your employees, they make no sense because the customer is *not* always right.

I believe fully in these two statements: ***The customer is not always right but is always the customer. The customer comes second.*** If you'll put your employees first, you won't have to worry about your customers. And if you can deal with angry customers in a healthy manner, you'll have a better chance at winning them as a "customer for life." When done well, you'll have "customers for life and employees for life."

The person outside my home does not come first. My wife comes first. And if she comes first, I won't have to worry about our relationships outside the home. My spouse is going to know she comes first in my life.

The other kids in the neighborhood don't come first. The teacher doesn't come first. My kid comes first. But the teacher is always the teacher, and the coach is always the coach, so I'm going to treat the teacher and coach with honor and respect. But my kids are going to know they come first in my life.

The seven-step process discussed in this chapter will help you to deal with angry people in a way that can restore the relationship and enable you to keep a customer for life, keep a spouse for life, maintain a strong relationship with your children, and keep your friendships intact.

18

THE W.A.D.E.L. MODEL FOR EFFECTIVE MEETINGS

THE TOOL I AM ABOUT TO SHARE WITH YOU is one that I ask you to be very careful with. Because people like it so much, they sometimes use it in the wrong way. This tool is not intended to be used to control or manipulate people. It's intended to strengthen relationships, communication, and productivity in your organization. It's called the W.A.D.E.L. model, and it's a tool to help you have effective meetings.

W.A.D.E.L.

W = Welcome

The "W" stands for *welcome*. At this stage of the meeting, it's time to share some good news. I say, "Tell me something good going on," "What's something fun you did over the weekend?", or "What's something positive going on in your life?"

As I have coached many kids' sports teams, I have used the W.A.D.E.L. model with the players. Coaches, referees, and parents from the other teams would come to me and ask, "How do you get nine-year-old kids to do this kind of stuff? To run these plays? To play this kind of defense? They're nine years old. How many times a week do you practice?"

We would practice one time a week for 50 minutes. During the first five to seven minutes of our practice times, the kids would get stuff off their minds. I'd say, "Tell me something good."

"It's my birthday this week."

"I made an A on my test."

"My grandmom is coming over."

When all that stuff was off their minds, they could focus totally on the practice for the sport being played.

That's the way adults are, too. When they get that opportunity to share what's on their minds, they're far more focused on the meeting at hand. Over time, it saves time for you and your people.

During the *welcome* stage, also do some affirmations. When you're meeting at work or having a meal, affirm people on your team. When you're meeting with your family, affirm your children and your spouse. Affirm them for something they've done. Thank them for something they've done.

Open the meeting on a positive note with good news and affirmations.

A = Ask questions

Then, it's time to *ask questions*. This is a very important part of the model. You might open the meeting by saying, "Here's the agenda for the meeting… Is there anything else anyone might want to add to the agenda?" This doesn't mean you must get to everything that might be added, but it means you started the meeting by inviting their feedback. You might ask, "Are there any needs any of you have today that we might not be aware of?" If it's the first time you're meeting the person, consider saying, "Tell me your story."

If you'll spend 2-4 minutes asking questions early in the meeting, you'll give people an opportunity to get things off their minds that they might have walked into the room with, enabling them to engage more fully in the meeting.

It would be easy to assume that the W.A.D.E.L. would make meetings longer rather than shorter. The reason it saves time is because people get to give input before the discussion part officially begins. Most of us are used to meetings where all kinds of things are swirling around in the minds of the attendees, preventing them from fully engaging with the specific items on the discussion agenda. This often derails the agenda and slows down the meeting. But if you can get that swirl out of their minds before starting the discussion, you'll have a more productive and efficient meeting.

D = Discussion

Now, it's time to enter the *discussion* portion of the meeting. In a one-on-one meeting, it might be a sales call, a family discussion, or a sports practice. But in a organizational meeting, there's normally an agenda to be discussed.

E = Empower

After the discussion, it's time to *empower* the people in the room to go out and fulfill their roles in what we discussed. Empower the people before they leave the room to make sure each person knows what he or she is supposed to do. When everyone returns to the next meeting, they can report back on how they've done.

L = Launch

As you empower the people with whom you are meeting, combine that with the *launch*. The launch is an encouraging story, poem, or video that inspires and motivates the people to do what they agreed to do. Someone other than the meeting facilitator can be assigned to share the launch message. Make sure the people are encouraged as they leave the meeting to fulfill their roles that contribute to the vision or goals of the organization.

Use the W.A.D.E.L. with the right motivations.

This model is intended to build relationships. It can work phenomenally well when you're using it with the right motivations. It can facilitate a great family dinner. It works well for any team meetings you have.

At the same time, if you abuse it to get people to do things for your personal benefit, people are going to see right through it, causing it to backfire. On the other hand, if you use this model genuinely to get feedback and build relationships, your team is going to get stronger, and the result will be higher performance. People will be able to tell the difference based on your attitude. During the affirmations part, they'll be able to tell if you're just flattering people or if you're genuinely affirming them. They'll know if you really mean it when you say, "Do you have any needs?" or "Do you want to add something to the agenda?" Are you just doing it to get through the process so you can get to the discussion? They'll be watching your body language and tone of voice.

What would a manipulative application of the W.A.D.E.L. model look like? A salesman might go into the meeting, do the welcome step, share something good, do some affirmation, and might even ask the question, "Now, tell me your story." But when he gets to the *discussion* part, the first thing he does is to get out his brochures and make it all about making the sale, not about building the relationship. So, the salesman *only* used the W.A.D.E.L. to sell his product.

We must be careful not to use the relational part of the W.A.D.E.L. just to get the transaction done because that's not being very relational or relactional. That's being solely transactional and manipulative.

Use this model to build relationships. When your relationships are strong, the sales will increase because the team is going to work together.

What does the W.A.D.E.L. model look like in action?

I have seen the W.A.D.E.L. work in one industry after another. When I started teaching this, I was told that there was no way this would work with certain age groups or in certain industries. One of those was the banking industry.

I had taken the staff at a mergers and acquisitions company through the Transformational Leadership training back in 2007. The president of that company asked me, "Ford, what do you think we need to change about our company to be successful long term? What do see you coming?"

I responded, "I don't think you'll want to hear what I have to say."

He assured me, "We really do."

I said, "Well, the problem is we're about to go through the worst economic recession that we've had since the Great Depression. The stock market is going to go down by 50%. In your industry right now, you're doing well because the mergers and acquisition industry is probably doing as well as it has ever done in the history of the United States. Because of that, there are many other things you do well that the bankers, CPAs, and lawyers have forgotten you do well because you're so successful in the industry. I would start reminding those bankers, CPAs, and lawyers about that. Tell them, "Hey, if you need this kind of work, be sure to give us a call."

The next year, the stock market did go down by about 50%. When it did, this relatively mid-sized M&A firm started reducing its staff because there weren't any mergers or acquisitions going on at the time. There wasn't enough money to buy or sell confidently because the value of money and the value of the stock market had dropped so significantly.

In the midst of this, that company's chief financial officer called me and said, "Ford, I've got a problem. I'm using your W.A.D.E.L. model with our clients, and it's flat out not working."

I said, "Then, I'm not sure you're using it."

He replied, "Would you go with me to call on a client?"

"I'd be happy to."

So, we went to a bank he had been calling on. This CFO had worked in this bank for many years earlier in his career, and they loved him. But they weren't giving him any business. I agreed to join him with the senior officer of the workout department to discuss the type of business I had recommended they start pursuing before the stock market crash. The workout department's responsibility is to work delinquent loans out of the bank. Many companies' and individuals' debts had been moved from the loan department to the workout department during this season because so many people were defaulting on their debts.

When we arrived for our meeting with the senior officer, his administrative assistant took us into his office. I then began the W.A.D.E.L. process. He was not there when we arrived.

When we entered his office, I started observing the pictures on his walls. You can often tell what is important to people by what they hang on their walls. I noticed some pictures of his family, which provided some valuable information about him and what was important to him.

A few minutes later, he came in and introduced himself briefly and started to guide us toward the board room where his associates were waiting.

I said, "Before we go down there, could you do me a favor?"

He said, "Yes."

Pointing toward one of his pictures with a lot of different people in it, I asked, "Could you tell me about this picture?" He spent the next 20 minutes telling me about each individual in that picture.

After he finished with that picture, I asked, "Hey, this picture over here... Is this your daughter?"

"It is," he said.

"Does she play AAU basketball?"

"Yeah."

I said, "My daughter does, too. Tell me what team she's on." He told me all about it.

About 30 minutes into our one-hour meeting, he looked up and said, "Oh, my... My two guys have been waiting on us in the board room for 30 minutes. We've got to go."

When we arrived in the board room, we introduced ourselves, and I started asking them, "Tell me about your career here... How long have you been here?" "I noticed you've got a wedding ring... Tell me about your family." The first guy spent about 10 minutes telling me about his career and family.

The second guy? Same thing.

About 55 minutes into our one-hour meeting, the senior vice president looked at me and said, "Hang on... Tom brought you here today to introduce us to you to find out what it is that you do that is so unique and different from other consultants. But you haven't said one word about yourself or your organization."

I said, "That's okay. Today, I just wanted to get to know you. Could we set up a second meeting for me to come back? At that meeting, I'll share with you who we are."

He said, "Is there any way that, in two minutes, you could tell me anything at all that would give me some hint about what you can do for us?"

It is very difficult to explain what we do in two minutes. I'm not sure exactly what I said. I wish I'd recorded it.

The senior vice president of this large bank looked at me and said, "I have a question for you."

"What's that?"

He said, "Can you teach my wife how to love me more?"

"Actually, I can," I replied.

His two employees laughed at him jokingly. He looked at them and said, "Look, I know you have a meeting now. I do, too. We're going to cancel our meetings. I want you to go to your office, and I want you to bring back all the companies we need help with. We're going to go through them and see how many he can take."

When that happened, Tom said, "Hang on... What just happened here?"

I said, "While you're getting your companies, I'll explain it to him."

After they left, I said, "Tom, I couldn't take any of these companies right now even if I wanted to. I came to get to know these guys and to see if I could help you and if they needed the kind of help that you can offer. I don't know what I'm going to tell them when they offer me this work, but let's work on it. You've been showing so much desperation. You've been using the W.A.D.E.L. model to make a sale. You haven't been using it to be in relationship."

When they came back in, they dropped a pile of these companies' files on the table and asked us to go through them. After we had gone through them for about 45 minutes, we picked out five companies who I thought could use the kind of help that Tom's company offered. I looked at Tom and said, "How about these five?"

They said, "Take them all."

I didn't have the time available to help these companies in the ways they needed to be helped. I said, "Is there any chance that you'd let Tom and his company have these?"

They said, "Absolutely. Tom, you take them."

Astonished, he said, "What?"

I said, "Tom, here are some new clients. Take them."

Our meeting had nearly concluded when the senior officer looked at me and said, "Earlier today, I asked you a question, and I was serious about it."

By this point, he had asked quite a few questions, so I said, "Which one?"

"I asked you if you could teach my wife how to love me more."

I said, "Well, I told you the answer, and I was serious. Your guys laughed at you, but I can teach your wife how to love you more."

He said, "So, if I give her your card with your phone number and she calls you, you'll talk to her and help her love me more?"

I looked at him and said, "Sir, I don't ever need to meet her." I didn't need to meet her to teach her how to love him more. He was the only one I needed to meet with to teach her how to love him more.

It's amazing what the W.A.D.E.L. model can accomplish when used to build relationships rather than to advance our own agenda.

Part 4

RELACTIONAL
TEAM PERFORMANCE

19

V.S.T.T.E.E.L.E. and Lead

WHAT KIND OF LEADER would you want to follow? What are those desired qualities and skills of a great leader? Make your own list and see what you come up with. Here are some examples of these traits that may be on your list:

- Visionary
- Caring
- Good communicator
- Humble
- Consistent
- Decisive
- Good delegator
- Empowers people

- Wisdom
- Compassionate
- High integrity
- Approachable
- Good listener
- Enthusiastic
- Teachable
- Good sense of humor

Wouldn't you want to follow a leader who had all these qualities listed above? If you exuded these qualities, wouldn't other people want to follow you? Certainly, yes!

Let's start to frame these qualities into a definition of an ideal leader. Perhaps your definition wouldn't describe who you are now or any person you've ever known, but what is your definition of the *ideal* leader?

I would suggest to you that **leaders are those who lay down their lives to serve those they influence**. When I say "lay down their lives," I don't mean that they die. This means they're willing to set aside their personal desires to take on a greater purpose. When we combine those qualities and skills alongside this definition and add the purpose below, we can become leaders with far more influence than we have ever dreamed of. This is to "V.S.T.T.E.E.L.E. and lead." Let's unpack this model.

V.S.T.T.E.E.L.E.

V = Vision

Leaders cast *vision*. An organization needs a clearly identified and compelling vision that people are inspired to follow.

S = Serve

After the vision has been cast, it is the leader's responsibility to serve and to "see to it that" the followers are taught, trained, and equipped so they can be empowered to accomplish their roles in fulfilling the shared vision.

T = Teach

Leaders are responsible for providing *knowledge* that the followers need to perform their roles in moving the organization toward the vision.

T = Train

Leaders must train their followers, which means providing them with the *experience* they need to perform before fully giving them the responsibility to do it.

E = Equip

To equip is to provide the *tools* necessary for your followers to perform at the highest level.

Before we move forward, let's clarify the difference between teaching, training, and equipping team members. *Teaching* provides new knowledge. *Training* provides experience. *Equipping* provides the actual tools to perform.

As an example, let's say you want your people to be taught, trained, and equipped on how to use an iPhone as well as multiple iPhone applications. If you brought them into a room and presented a bunch of PowerPoint presentations and a manual to show them how to use it, that would be *teaching*.

If an iPhone was given to each person and they were allowed to practice what they're reading in the manual and seeing in the PowerPoint presentations, that would be *training*.

If after all of the teaching and training they were sent back to work with an iPhone, that would be *equipping*.

E = Empower

When the follower has the knowledge (teaching), experience (training), and tools (equipping) to succeed, we can fully *empower* the person to do the job, which leads to more capacity for the leader and the organization.

At times, we think we're *empowering* people when we're merely *delegating* tasks. But if we empower people before we've taught, trained, and equipped them, we can get them and our organizations into trouble. Delegation is a precursor to empowerment. This is a part of the teaching, training, and equipping.

Let's assume I have a new administrative assistant. He or she comes to work on Monday morning, and I tell the person that one of the responsibilities is to handle my calendar. I explain that, on this Thursday, I have four people coming in for lunch. They will arrive at 11:30 a.m. I ask my new administrative assistant to bring in three pizzas—a meat pizza, a veggie pizza, and a cheese pizza—a Diet Coke, a Sprite, and a couple of salads with some ranch dressing. I then provide the name and phone number of the pizza place. That is *delegation*.

What does *empowerment* look like?

Let's turn the clock forward 90 days. Over this time, I have taught, trained, and equipped this person to know how to manage my calendar. On Monday morning, the person comes into my office and says, "I noticed on your calendar you have four people coming in for lunch. Are there any special dietary needs?"

I'll say, "No. Thank you for checking."

Soon thereafter, the person tells me, "Your lunch will be here at 11:30 a.m."

Now, that's what empowerment is.

Later, perhaps the person will tap on the door, stick his or her head in, and say, "By the way, if you had put it on your calendar that there were no special dietary needs, I wouldn't have had to bother you." The training should go both ways to help us perform our jobs more effectively. When the relationship is strong, this sort of two-way training can happen.

L = Let go

Once you have empowered the person who has the requisite knowledge, experience, and tools, you can confidently *let go* and allow the person to fulfill his or her responsibility, moving toward the common vision.

E = Evaluate

At this point, the job of the leader becomes to *evaluate* the person's performance in light of your clearly defined expectations and the vision for the organization. It is important that they know and understand how they are doing in their roles in relation to the shared vision.

V.S.T.T.E.E.L.E. to reduce stress in your organization.

Think about a time when you may have sent one of your team members to do something before that person was taught, trained, and equipped. It could have been your employee, your child, or someone else. How did that go? What was your stress level like during that experience?

Now, how about a time when you sent one of your team members to accomplish something only after you first taught, trained, and equipped that person for the task?

Which experience was more productive? Less stressful?

Based on the V.S.T.T.E.E.L.E. model, what is the quality of your leadership today? Where do you want to be? Are you a teacher, trainer, and equipper? Are you empowering? Have you been delegating before or after your people have been taught, trained, and equipped? If you've been delegating before the person is ready, you may be stressed, and your team member and his or her co-workers may also be stressed as a result.

As you lead, go through the V.S.T.T.E.E.L.E. model. Leadership becomes much easier and less stressful when we have teams around us who are empowered because we've taught, trained, and equipped them.

Cast a compelling vision. Serve. Teach. Train. Equip. Empower. Let go. Evaluate. As a result, you will become a highly influential, relational, and transformational leader.

20

How Healthy Is Your Organization?

So far in this book, we have been discussing the tools of relational leadership that can help you to enhance the performance of your organization. Now, let's assess the current health of your organization.

Assessing and Building Trust

Building trust is one of the main challenges in building high-performing teams with strong personal relationships and high individual performance. Some people in your organization will find it more difficult than most to trust you and their co-workers. They are on one end of the *trust continuum*. These people have very low or no trust until we give them a reason to trust us.

On the other end of the continuum are people who will have a high level of trust and some who will even trust 100% until given a reason not to.

As you look at the trust continuum, put your initials on the graph where you imagine yourself. Now, put the initials of each person on your team.

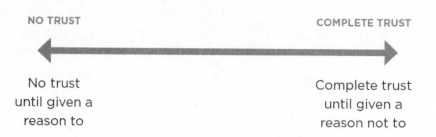

NO TRUST

COMPLETE TRUST

No trust
until given a
reason to

Complete trust
until given a
reason not to

Where there is low trust, there will be lower overall performance and unhealthy relationships. Where there is a high level of trust, there will at least be healthy relationships, and if we've done a good job with teaching, training, equipping, and putting the people in the right places, we will also have high individual performance.

Assessing Performance and Relationship Health

Now, imagine a team that you are on. Assess the performance levels of each person on your team, including yourself. Place your initials in the spot on this graph that corresponds with each person on your team. Are they high performers with healthy relationships? High performers with unhealthy relationships? Low performers with healthy relationships? Low performers with unhealthy relationship?

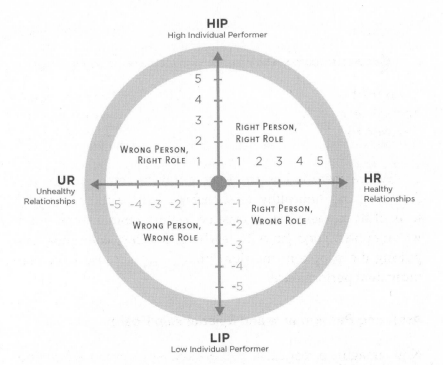

Everyone in the upper right-hand quadrant, your high individual performers and healthy relationships people, would be considered either inner core or core. I call this having the *right person* in the *right role*.

If you have people in the lower right-hand quadrant, which means they have healthy relationships but low performance, those people need job training. If you put them in roles with responsibilities they can't fulfill, that's not their fault. But if you put them in roles where they can thrive, consider sending them for some training to help teach, train, and equip them in a better way so they can move into the upper right-hand quadrant. I call this quadrant having the *right person* in the *wrong role*.

People in the upper left-hand quadrant are high performers with unhealthy relationships. What kind of training do they need? They need relational training. They may need anger management. You know who they are. This the *wrong person* in the *right role*.

People in the lower left-hand quadrant are low individual performers with unhealthy relationships. I recommend you deal with those people quickly. This is the *wrong person* in the *wrong role*.

Where are your people on the graph? Where is your team collectively? Wherever the lowest performer and most-unhealthy-relationship person is, that's where the team is. If you have one person down in the lower left-hand quadrant, a low performer with unhealthy relationships, this is making a major negative impact on the overall team. The goal is to get everyone on your team into the upper right-hand quadrant.

Inner Core, Core, Lean-Inners, and Lean-Outers

Every organization I've ever owned, consulted with, or been involved with in some other way—whether businesses, schools, families, governments, or churches—has had four distinct groups of people. When you understand those four groups and how they impact the organization, it becomes much easier to know how to deal with them.

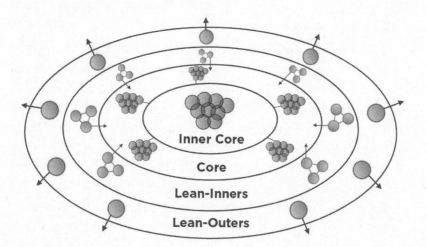

The first group is the *inner core*. Typically, this would be the management or leadership team. The inner core consists of those on the team who have bought into the vision. They're going after it wholeheartedly.

The next concentric circle of people around the inner core is a group called the *core*. These people may not be in those management meetings or in the vision meetings, but they're totally bought in. More than likely, they report to someone who is in the inner core. They're moving forward with you.

The challenge is there are two other groups in every organization I've ever seen. The first one is called the *lean-inners*. They're looking in and saying, "Wow, I think I want to be a part of that." But, for some reason, they're not quite ready to jump in all the way. Why might that be? Maybe it's a hippocampus issue. Maybe they're thinking, *I've seen this before, and I'm not convinced they're going to finish.* Maybe it's something else like a trust issue. They're waiting for you to build a little more trust before they say, "I'm all in." But they're thinking about it.

The fourth group is the problem. Those are the *lean-outers*. They're the ones who have no intention of ever getting in. They're the ones who pull the pin and toss the grenade into the middle of the group. Why do they do that? Because right now, they control the culture, and they don't want to give up the control.

Fortunately, it only takes 3% to 15% of any organization to shift the culture. Unfortunately, it takes 3% to 15% of the organization to shift the culture. So, every leader must ask, "Which 3% to 15% is controlling the culture in this organization?" If you allow a lot of lean-outers to stay in your organization, the lean-inners will join them by becoming lean-outers. Sometimes, the lean-inners will refuse to get in because they don't trust that the inner core and core will deal with the lean-outers. When we remove the lean-outers or get them to lean into the core, the lean-inners will then jump into the core.

What would happen if you had an organization that had no lean-outers and almost no lean-inners but a lot of inner core and core? You'd have higher performance and healthier relationships among your team.

Unfortunately, the lean-outers will often be some of your top performers. Nevertheless, they are dragging down your organization. Have you ever noticed that most organizations write almost all of their policies and procedure manuals based on the lean-outers? Refer back to the chapter on "How to Discipline" either to lean the lean-outers totally out of your organization or lean them into the core. You can allow them to make the choice: 1) get on board or 2) find another organization.

Have you ever been hard at work while the person on your team next to you wasn't working hard, so you thought, *What difference does it make whether I work hard or not?*

Have you ever worked in an organization in which you tried to have a good attitude, but someone around you (maybe a group of people) didn't have a good attitude? Nobody dealt with that person's bad attitude, so you thought, *Why should I be the only one keeping a good attitude?* Then, you and others around you exchanged your good attitudes for bad ones?

Maybe you were the one who was always on time for work, but one of your teammates came in 15 minutes late every day. You started questioning, *Why do I have to be at work on time?*

In scenarios like these, it becomes easy for good people to drop into that lean-outer category.

Leaning Out a Lean-Outer

Our company once bought a company that was doing about $60 million in sales annually, but they were not doing well. Our intention was to buy this company, fix it, turn it around, build a management team, and let that management team run the company using the tools I have been sharing with you in this book.

On our first day working in this company, we were teaching many of these relactional leadership concepts. During a break about halfway through the day, the vice president of sales called me into her office. When I entered, she threw her keys on the table, signaling her resignation.

I picked up her keys and gently said, "Okay. Clean out your office and be out of here by five o'clock today."

"What?" she asked.

I asked her, "Why did you throw your keys on the table?"

She said, "That means I quit."

I said, "Well, that means you don't have a job anymore. So, go ahead and clean your office."

She said to me, "You can't do this without me. Do you realize that, out of the $60 million in sales we have, I personally generate $55 million of that? Those are *my* relationships?"

I said, "Sure, I know that. We did our due diligence before we bought the company."

"Well, your way won't work," she said.

I was thinking, *We wouldn't be here if your way was working. We bought your company because your way hasn't been working.* I said, "Then, why would you want to work here? If my way won't work, you should go ahead and leave. And I'm okay with that, so go ahead and clean your office."

She then started crying and said, "Where will I ever find another job that pays me $250,000 a year in base pay plus commission?"

"You probably won't," I said. She started pleading for another chance. "You know… You just met me today, so I'm going to do something for you I've never done before. I'm going to give your keys back with two stipulations. Number one: If you ever throw them on the table again, you're gone. Number two: If I ever hear from anybody that I gave your keys back, including your mother, you're gone. We don't do business this way. We don't accept it. We do something totally different than that."

She said, "I got it."

About three months later, guess what she did. In a moment of anger, she threw her keys on the table again. I guess her epinephrine kicked in. I immediately grabbed her keys. In an attempt to grab her keys before I did, she scratched my hand. I said, "Young lady, you're gone. We do not do business this way." Remember she made the choice when she threw the keys on the table. I did not make it for her. I told her that, if she ever did that again, it would be over.

Within about three months of her being gone, we reduced the sales by $5 million and increased the profits by 11%.

Many times, those lean-outers are the problem. But the previous owner and president believed there would be no way the company could succeed without her because she had been generating so many sales. In reality, she was a problem.

If we deal with those lean-outers, the lean-inners will jump into the core, and your organization will reach a new level of effectiveness.

21

CONFRONTING CONSTRAINTS

ANYTHING THAT MOVES YOU toward fulfilling a goal of your organization is considered *productive*. If you're leading within a for-profit company, one of your goals would likely be to generate profit. In a nonprofit or within a family, the goal would be defined in other ways.

How productive is your organization? How can you make your organization more productive?

One of my favorite teachings on how to solve these problems is called the theory of constraints (TOC), which was developed by Dr. Eliyahu Goldratt.[4] I highly recommend that you read his book titled *The Goal* and see how his teachings can help you to solve constraints in your organization. Below are some teachings and expansions on his teachings about his theory of constraints.

There are certain tangible and intangible things that must be channeled through your organization's system in order to achieve your organization's goal. As labeled by Dr. Goldratt, these items are called *throughput*. For a company, it's the rate at which a system generates money. I have expanded on his definition for it to fit any kind of organization:

> Throughput is the rate at which a system generates money (or whatever the goal is), from the time an idea is conceived until it reaches its final user, is paid for, and is not returned.

Your organization's rate of throughput is the first measurement of productivity.

On the other hand, a *constraint* is anything that inhibits or stops throughput. It is any resource that cannot produce the demand placed on it. There are two types of constraints.

First, there are *personal* constraints that we all have as leaders. Remember that *"no organization can move beyond the constraints of its leadership."*

The second category of constraints is *processes, policies, systems, and procedures.* *"No organization can move beyond the constraints of its processes, policies, systems, or procedures."* Typically, these are defined by the leader, so the leader has direct control of these types of constraints.

In addition to throughput, a second way to measure productivity is *inventory,* which consists of all the items we have purchased for the purpose of selling.

The third measurement of productivity is *operational expense,* which consists of all the money we spend turning that inventory into throughput.

What does all of this look like in action?

Let's assume we want to sell a printed t-shirt. What's the *throughput*? As we invest time and expertise to decide on the color of the shirt, the logo on the shirt, and the quality of the shirt, we are investing throughput to help us reach our goal of selling that shirt. We continue adding throughput as the shirt's design goes through the production department, to the shipping department, and to a retailer where it must be sold. At that point, the goal has only been accomplished if the customer pays for it and doesn't return it. If there is a return, the throughput does not fully take place.

If you are running a business, understanding the concept of throughput will help you to price your products and services properly as well as to enhance the quality of your work to minimize returns.

What might throughput look like in a family? It depends what the goal is. Let's say that your goal is for your child to graduate from college, get a job, and be a successful participant in society. So, all the money you spend getting the child born is inventory expense. All the money you spend raising and training that child and getting him or her through college would be operational expense. If the child actually graduated from college, got a job, became self- sufficient, and contributed to society for the rest of his or her life, you have achieved the goal. If your child drops out and returns home or quits his or her job and returns home, then throughput stops and the goal has not been achieved.

If the goal of a church or synagogue is to make disciples, all the money spent getting people into the organization and into the discipleship program would be called inventory expense. All the money spent training the people would be operational expense. If a person receives the training, becomes a disciple, and remains a disciple until death, the goal has been achieved. If he or she doesn't remain a disciple, the goal has not been achieved and throughput is not accomplished.

Two Types of Phenomena in Achieving the Goal

There are two challenging phenomena that you will face as you aim to remove constraints that hinder you from helping your organization to reach its goals.

The first one is *dependent events*, which means that one event must take place before another event can occur. For example, you can't put print a logo on a t-shirt until you've purchased the t-shirt on which the logo must be printed. That's a dependent event.

You'll also experience *statistical fluctuations*. This means the process remains the same but is requiring different amounts of time and effort to complete each cycle.

For example, let's assume you have a goal of arriving at work within a specific amount of time each morning. If you took the same path to work every day, the travel time could vary based on the sequence of the red lights, the weather, how fast or slow the drivers are, an accident, getting pulled over for a ticket, etc. That's a statistical fluctuation.

In order to reach the goals of our organizations, the key is to remove the bottlenecks, the constraints in our organizations. How can we do that?

Five-Step Process for Removing the Constraints

Now, let's identify the steps to confronting/removing the constraints that hinder the effectiveness of your organization.

1: Identify the biggest constraint.

This is often the hardest part of removing a constraint. But, if you can identify the biggest one, you'll notice that many things you thought were your biggest problems are merely symptoms of that constraint.

2: Exploit the constraint.

Get or squeeze everything you can out of that constraint. Once you've done this, it's likely that you will have removed the constraint. Then, you can go back to step one and identify the next biggest constraint.

3: Subordinate everything else.

If step two didn't work, all your other leadership decisions should be focused on removing the constraint you identified in step one. Everything in the organization that is not a constraint (bottleneck) is now subordinated to the constraint (bottleneck).

4: Elevate the constraint.

If step three doesn't work, place even greater importance on understanding the constraint by researching and dissecting that constraint into its smallest intricacies. Examine them in as much detail as possible to figure out how to break the constraint.

5: Break the constraint.

At any point in the process, you may find that you have broken the constraint. When this happens, go back to step one and identify the next biggest constraint.

As you remove these bottlenecks, you'll find that your organization's production will flow much smoother. In a family, there will be significantly less stress. In a religious organization or nonprofit, people will want to be there more. As you see this happening, you'll want to remain in this process of constantly identifying constraints in your organization. As a result, you'll also knock out the problems that are actually just symptoms of the actual constraint.

I once applied this theory to my wife and marriage just as I did in companies and other organizations. After applying the process, I didn't like what I found. Sandra's biggest constraint was me! So, all we had to do was get me fixed to have an awesome marriage.

22

THE FIVE ORGANIZATIONAL MODELS

HAVE YOU EVER been or been around a leader who had a domineering leadership style? If so, you were (or are) seeing someone who likes to be in complete control of the whole organization, which can lead to distress, anxiety, and anger. It can cause such people to hurt those they lead.

Have you ever been around a leader like the one I just described who had a change of heart that resulted in a change in his or her leadership style? Sometimes, people like this have a change of heart and revert to a gentle and kind style of leadership. When that happens, their organizations often are not as effective or productive as they were under their dominant style of leadership. As a result, they revert to their old style to get things under control. Once things are under control, they return to being gentle and kind again. Then, they go back to being controlling.

What I have described above is what I call a *schizophrenic leadership* style. Leaders who aren't balanced in their approach tend to hurt their people, which hurts the organizations they lead.

The Visionary Model: Leader Casts Vision

Most leaders default to either one of two models. The first is sometimes referred to as the *top-down* or *command-and-control* model. It's the one that says everything must go through the leader. I do not want to throw this model out. I want to re-name it and call it the *Visionary Model*.

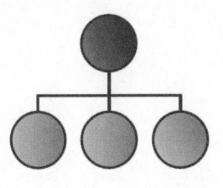

The Servant Leadership Model: Serve, Teach, Train, and Equip

The second one is the *servant leadership* model. This one often doesn't work very well either because it's often dysfunctional. People may be getting along for a period of time. However, conflict eventually comes and is often not dealt with properly as many servant leadership models have little-to-no accountability with their staff or volunteers, so dysfunction sets in, conflict still arises, and the organization becomes unproductive.

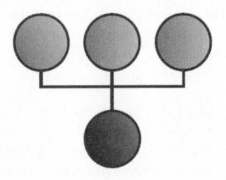

The Functional Responsibility Model: Delegate and Empower

If we combined the best aspects of both the *visionary* model and the *servant leadership* model, I call this the *functional responsibility* model.

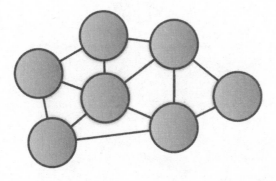

In this model, the CEO is still the CEO. The department manager is still the department manager. The mom and dad are still the mom and dad. The church pastor is still the pastor. The rabbi is still the rabbi. The coach is still the coach. The classroom teacher is still the teacher. They're trying to gain consensus through this model, but if they can't, they're still responsible for making the decision. The roles and responsibilities remain clear, but they're connected through relationship. In the diagram above, the skinnier and the longer the line, the less of a relationship there is. The closer and fatter the line, the closer the relationship.

The Relational Model: Empower and Let Go

The *functional responsibility* model develops into a fourth model called the *relational* model. In this model, the transactional approach and the relational approach we've been discussing in this book start coming together. It requires that the relationships are healthy and that people understand their roles and have the ability to fulfill them. When this happens, the sales department wants to work alongside the manufacturing department. In other organizations, areas in conflict can now work together because they realize the organization will be much stronger when they are working together than in a top-down or bottom-up approach.

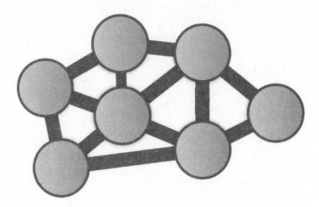

The Continuous Improvement Model: Evaluate

If we stay in the *relactional* model long enough, those circles will begin to intersect and overlap one another. When this happens, the people start caring as much about the other departments and their success as they do their own. They start communicating, and when they communicate and start caring about one another, the *relactional* model develops into a *continuous improvement* model. Now, we're looking forward to grow the organization instead of always looking backward.

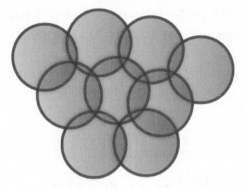

Growing from One Model to the Next

As we cast vision, serve, teach, train, equip, empower, let go, and evaluate (V.S.T.T.E.E.L.E.), we are helping our organizations to grow through these models. The stress levels will drop. The team will be functioning together far better than they would if they were being yelled at or neglected. In this model, people are held accountable. Job descriptions are clear. Everybody is moving forward together.

As an example, what would these organizational models look like in the sales and production departments of a business?

Let's start with the *command-and-control* model. The boss has dictated the price and the delivery date. The salesman goes out and presents the price and terms to the customer, but the customer says, "I need it at a lower price."

The salesman returns to his boss with the customer's feedback. The boss says, "You can sell it for less, and you can sell it with a faster delivery time."

The order proceeds to the production department. They look at their schedule and say, "There's no way we can deliver on time." Now, we have a fight going on as there's a constant tension between sales and operations on delivery time and price.

What would this look like in the *servant leadership* model? The salesman wants to sell it, so he sells it at a price that is too low and at a delivery time that is too fast. The boss doesn't hold them accountable. When the production department receives the order, they say, "I don't have to meet that delivery time. It's not a big deal. We'll just work it into the schedule whenever we can." *Boom!* Conflict arises, and the order is not delivered on time.

What would this look like in the *functional responsibility* model? They would start to realize that the problem is they're not getting along very well and that they don't have clarity concerning their roles. Now that relationships and communication are being developed, they will begin to discuss who has the ultimate authority for setting the price and delivery date. Some of the same mistakes will be made, but they will be fewer and farther between.

How about the *relational* model? The team starts to realize they must communicate with one another. They must take confidence in knowing everyone is in the right place. They must trust that everyone is doing what's best for the organization. Apologies are made when communication breakdowns happen, and the team members take responsibility for and learn from their mistakes.

The relational model then flows into the *continuous improvement* model. Now, meetings are happening before sales calls are made and before the production schedule is finalized. Decisions are made together. When there are unresolved disagreements, the CEO steps in and makes the call. As a result of this teamwork, time is saved, sales go up, production gets faster, and the company gains and maintains more clients.

In a non-profit, the employees and volunteers will be happier and better contributors. On a sports team, the players and coaches will win more games together and have healthier relationships. In a religious organization, the staff will be happier and more productive, and the members will want to participate in more of its services and programs. In a family, the spouses get along better, which leads to better relationships and better examples for their kids, and they start performing at higher levels.

Relactional leadership leads to continuous improvement in organizations. Now, let's explore how teams can reach a state of continuous improvement by growing through these five organizational models.

23

THE FIVE STAGES OF
TEAM-BUILDING

A FEW YEARS AGO, I received a voicemail from our athletic director. He said, "Ford, I need a favor. Our volleyball coach has quit. I know you've never coached volleyball, and I know you don't have time, but would you take on the varsity volleyball team?"

I called him back and said, "Hey, Tom. This is Ford. Let me answer your question: I don't have time, and I've never coached volleyball. What's up?"

He said, "Well, as you know, we have no returning seniors and only one returning starter. Our coach left, and we are projected to place last in the league. I don't have time to go out and recruit and find a new coach."

I said, "Okay, so keep going."

He said, "At some point, I would love to get what you're doing into our school system by showing the results it can produce on a volleyball team. I think I'll be able to do that."

I said, "Okay, let me talk to my daughter." My daughter was the one returning starter, so I needed to talk to her to see if she wanted me to be the coach. She said "yes," and I accepted the role.

Driving home on the third night of practice, my daughter said to me, "Dad, are you sure you want to do this?" I had coached many different sports with our daughters and had experienced some decent success, but she knew this was going to be tough.

I said to her, "Darling, don't worry. On Saturday, we're going to bring the team together for a day, and we're going to start walking through this stuff. And as we walk through it, I'm going to teach these kids the tools we teach in companies, schools, and churches. We may not have a winning season, but we will still have a good season. But, next year, we should win some matches."

I also had some secret weapons: Two assistant coaches who did know the game of volleyball and a daughter who would end up teaching me the game as we went. Throughout the season, my daughter actually coached *me* in the sport.

Stage 1: Visionary

That Saturday, we went through the W.A.D.E.L. model. We put a social covenant in place. I found out what their goals were. I taught them about their hippocampus issues and how their thoughts cause their feelings and actions (T.F.A.). I shared with them the differences between men's brains and women's brains. As we went through all of this, we deepened our social covenant. When conflict would arise during practice, we would pause to deal with it.

Our foundation was established from the beginning, which made us a tightly knit team going forward. We had a *vision* for where we wanted to go together as a team. They set a goal to win one match out of 23 to be played.

Stage 2: Servant Leadership

From there, we moved into the *servant leadership* stage. In this stage, I used the S.L.O.W.E.R. model of listening and the W.A.D.E.L. model to run the practices. I listened to them, first. At the beginning of our practices, the first thing I would do is to ask them to tell me something good that was going on in their lives. Then, I would do some affirmations.

I would ask the players to tell me something we did well and something we didn't do well at the previous practice.

Again, I had never coached volleyball. I would go home at night, and my daughter would teach me more about the game. She would teach me the options on how to set up the defense and how to run the offense. We had an assistant coach who understood volleyball. We had a plan for practice but usually would modify our practice schedule for the day based on the players' feedback. We'd say, "We might not get to all of this today, but we may get to some of it." Then, we'd begin the practice after everyone had an opportunity to share what they thought had been going well and what they thought hadn't been going so well.

Stage 3: Functional Responsibility

In this stage, we ensured that everyone had a clear understanding of each person's role on the team. Who would be an outside hitter? A middle hitter? A right-side hitter? Who would play defense? Who would be the captains? Role clarity was essential.

We taught the captains that they were the leaders. It was the captains' responsibility to help make the decisions of who would play where. They would learn how to deal with the team when people are upset. They were taught and helped to walk out the social covenant when conflict would arise.

With input from the team, the captains wrote the team's social covenant. It explained what would happen if a team member did not respect, care for, and honor another team member. They said, if that happened, they would go to the person one on one. If that didn't work, they would bring a teammate. If that didn't work, they would bring the issue before the entire team. If that didn't work, the person would be off the team.

They also wrote a social covenant for the parents of the players. They decided that—if one of their parents yelled at a referee, coach, or a player—that parent would have to miss one set, which is one game out of a best-of-five match. If they did it twice, they would have to miss a whole match. If they did it again, they would be out for the season and would have to pay for therapy. And they made their parents sign it.

Early in the season, we had a dad on the sideline who was yelling at his daughter, which was making her cry. I looked at him from the sidelines with my palms up in the air. When he saw me, he got up and walked out of the gym on his own. Because of our social covenant, he knew he had to sit out for a game. About two games later, he was yelling again. Once again, I looked at him from across the gym with my palms up in the air, and he walked out.

I found him after the match had ended and said, "You do understand that, if you yell one more time during the season, you're out for the season? You do understand that? Here's where you signed it. If you yell at your daughters one more time, you're out. I don't yell at them. You can't yell at them, and you agreed to that. I can't control what you do at home, but we all agreed not to yell at them at practice or in games."

I then said, "Oh, by the way… If you yell again, you'll also have to get paid professional counseling because that's what it says. I charge $1,000 an hour, and I would love to counsel you."

For the rest of the season, he didn't yell at them again.

Stage 4: Relational

What were the results of the team going through this process and acquiring these transformational leadership tools? This team was projected to win only one out of 23 matches that year, and remember that there were no returning seniors and only one returning starter.

But the team was now in the *relational* stage. Why? There was no threat within the team. Everybody on the team was taking responsibility for how they played. If they caused conflict, they accepted responsibility. They had learned how to apologize to one another.

In our last league match of the season, we were playing a team that had beat us badly the first time we played them that season. The winner of this match would get second place in our league. We couldn't find a team in the history of our school that had ever won second place. By now, our athletic director was getting phone calls from other athletic directors saying he had lied by telling them his volleyball coach had never coached volleyball before. (Remember I had a daughter and an assistant coach who understood volleyball.)

During the match, the other team won the first game, but we won the second game. In our previous match against this team, we never got close to winning a game. They won the third game, and we were in the fourth game out of five.

At one point in the fourth game, we were down by five points, and I called a timeout. When I would call a timeout, we would do things like dance in the huddle. I would give them very specific instructions on what to do to cover the floor and to change the game, but it was always done in an affirming way. I never yelled at them, and I told them I wouldn't. This way of treating people lowers their anxiety and helps them to perform at higher levels.

During the timeout, I said, "Hey, you see that coach over there?"

They said, "Yeah."

"She's mean," I said. And all the girls laughed. "Let me tell you something. If you'll go back out on that floor and dive for every ball and not let anything hit the floor… even if you don't win the point, they'll get frustrated. They are already frustrated that we even beat them in one game. They don't know what to do with that. They're supposed to dominate us, but we're in the match. If you can win these next five points, let me tell you what will happen. That coach will jump up, kick her chair, throw her clipboard, and start screaming at her players."

Early in the season, I had already explained to them how men's brains and women's brains work. I continued, "They'll go back to the last arguments they had with their boyfriend or their dad, or they'll go shopping, and they'll forget about volleyball." All the girls laughed. They went back out on the court.

I could not believe it, but they won the next five points. Sure enough, when they did, the other team's coach jumped up, yelled "timeout", and started screaming at her players.

During the timeout, I said, "We've got them. Go back out there right now and be waiting for them when they get back on the floor." We won that match.

That season, our team had the best record in the history of the school and won second place in the league to the number-one team in the league who was completely undefeated and, at one point, was the top-ranked team in the state in a bigger division than ours.

Stage 5: Continuous Improvement

During that season, one of the young ladies came to me and said, "Coach, can I share something with you?"

I said, "Yes, if your parents are okay with it."

I met privately with her while her parents were outside, and she shared with me some difficulties she had experienced when she was younger and that she believed it was a part of why she caused so much conflict. Why did she feel so free to share that with me? It was because she trusted me. I had shared my story with them about insecurities and how they had made me an arrogant person in high school as well as later in life. I had shared with them how it had impacted my family. So, she knew she had the freedom to share her story with me. I talked her through it and helped her deal with it better.

When a conflict arose about two weeks later, she raised her hand and said, "I'm the problem." She then shared her story with the team. After she had finished, three other teammates said they had also dealt with that and the insecurities that resulted from it.

After they had released those emotional burdens, they became better volleyball players. They became stronger as a team. They were now able to move into the *continuous improvement* stage. They could work together, practice together, plan together, and play together. They believed that everyone's opinion mattered. That little team of young ladies, high school students, went from a place where they didn't think they could win more than one match and won second place in their division.

These are the tools that helped us to win more. They can also help your organization to win more. Be intentional about using them no matter where you are leading.

For me, the best part of that season was getting to work alongside my daughter. While I had the skill set to teach the team how to get along and work together, I had little knowledge of the game of volleyball. When we would come home at night after practice, she would teach me about volleyball. At practice and at games, I would act like I knew what I was doing based on what she was teaching me at night. In the games, I would tell the girls, "If I tell you to do something and Quincy tells you something else, listen to her." I got a lot of credit for the winning record of that team, and my daughter got a lot of credit for being a great player. But the reality was, she was a great coach to me as well. What a fun experience to share with her.

Part 5

GROWING AS A
RELACTIONAL LEADER

24

V.P.M.O.S.A.:
Our Mission in Life

One day, Alfred Nobel picked up the newspaper and read that he had supposedly died when, in reality, it was his brother who had passed away. As he read what the newspaper said about him, he realized he would forever be remembered primarily as the man who created dynamite. He was going to be remembered as the man whose invention had killed people. He decided he didn't want to be remembered in this way.

So, what did he do about it? He came up with the Nobel Peace Prize so he would be remembered for peace rather than death and destruction.

As Alfred Nobel did, consider your legacy. This could be one of the most important things you will ever do. Take the time to write these things down.

1. What do you want your tombstone to say?
2. When you die, what do you want to be said about you at your funeral? How do you want your spouse, children, friends, and coworkers to remember you?
3. Based on your tombstone and obituary, what values should you be living out here and now?

After you've written these things down, embark on the V.P.M.O.S.A. process. You can do this for yourself on a personal level and then for your organization.

The V.P.M.O.S.A. Process

V = Vision

What future reality are you pursuing? What do you aspire to or dream of accomplishing? Where are you going as a leader? Write this down. This is your vision statement.

P = Purpose

Why would you pursue this vision? *Why* are you here? This is your purpose statement.

M = Mission

What are you willing to do that others may not be willing to do to bring your vision into reality? What sets you apart? That is your mission statement.

As you write out your vision, mission, and purpose statements, don't get bound up in the semantics of which one is the mission, which one is the purpose, and which one is the vision. Answer the reflection questions above to the best of your ability.

O = Objectives

Next, identify 2-3 objectives that you want to accomplish in the next 12-18 months to move you toward your vision, purpose, and mission. These objectives are your goals as a leader. After you get some experience in this process, I would write down 5-6 objectives on an annual or regular basis.

S = Strategies

Identify 2-3 strategies that can help you to fulfill each objective/goal.

A = Actions

Now, identify specific actions you need to take to implement each strategy within the next 12-18 months. What are the specific actions that would be measurable if you executed these strategies?

Again, don't get bound up in the semantics of whether something is an objective, strategy, or action step. Just write them down and go for it.

V.P.M.O.S.A. Application

This process will make it much easier for you to prioritize your life, causing your stress level to decrease significantly. It will help you to simplify your decision-making processes. When there's a request for your time and energy, you simply ask, "Will this help me to fulfill my vision? Would this type of activity line up with my vision, mission, and purpose? Would it impact what I want others to say about me at my funeral? Would it influence the words on my tombstone?"

As you prioritize your life and leadership in this way, people will observe your life and may say, "You're lucky." Luck is where the pathway of preparation intersects with the pathway of opportunity. Over time, as we are prepared and opportunity comes, we will see that these become points of destiny. It's really not about luck. It's about preparation meeting opportunity that moves us toward the destiny we desire.

People often tell me, "Ford, I wish I had done this V.P.M.O.S.A. process sooner." I can relate. The first time I went through this process, I ended up on the floor weeping as I compared what I had written down with what my life reflected in reality. Your life may not be as messed up internally as mine was, so you may not experience this. But, if you shed some tears, get comfortable with it. They can help with the healing process.

I'd encourage you to make getting this done a top priority. If you'll take the time to write this, you'll be able to look forward expectantly toward your vision. You'll also be able to look backward on your life and see that those points from your past may not have been good luck or bad luck. Most likely, they were points of destiny that were moving you toward the fulfillment of your written-down vision.

One of the things that's most important to me is my family. If I get a phone call asking me to travel to consult, teach, or train, the first thing I do is to check with my wife. What would this commitment do to your schedule? What would this do to our schedule? What would this do to my schedule? Do my children have any important activities that are so important to them that I should not miss them? If I don't live and lead like this, what I've written down as my epitaph and obituary won't happen.

25

ROAD TO NEVERLAND

MANY OF US CLAIM that there are certain things we'll *never* do. Almost always on that list is something we end up doing anyway. We end up making that treacherous fall or slip up that leads us off the path to "Neverland," a place we told ourselves we would never go. The road to Neverland is paved with good intentions as well as temptations and trials.

One of my Neverlands was that I was never going to get a divorce or cheat on my wife. From my perspective, as I was traveling for business, I was experiencing feelings of rejection, and the emotional distance between my wife and I began to grow. The traveling, feelings of rejection, and emotional distance continued to increase.

Soon, I began fantasizing about someone else who was not my wife. Inevitably, I acted on my fantasy and did the very thing I said I would never do.

We all have a "place" of who we aspire to be or how we want others to view us. That place is our *ideal selves*. On the other hand, there is that person who we really are, our *real selves*.

We all experience gaps between our ideal self and our real self. The bigger that gap gets, the bigger our stress gets as we try to hide what's really going on. When that stress kicks in, our bodies are like a car that's breaking down. When a car is full of gas, oil, and transmission fluid, and it has good tire pressure and strong belts, the car typically will drive well. But if any one of those things start failing, you'll have to pull the car over; otherwise, the engine could burn out or the car could break down in some other way.

From firsthand experience, I can tell you that running out of oil will eventually destroy your engine if you keep driving. If your tire gets flat, you can't keep driving. Our bodies are that way. When our bodies are fully fueled with serotonin, the stuff that keeps us in balance, we're probably sleeping well, exercising, and eating well. In this condition, our stress level is low.

Our bodies also need to be balanced with dopamine, which causes us to want to be in relationship with other people.

Once the gap between our ideal self, or who we put ourselves out to be, and our real self comes, stress hits our lives. When it does, our serotonin and dopamine levels become unbalanced. Our adrenal system gets completely out of whack, and our bodies start releasing shots of adrenaline when they're not supposed to.

If our adrenal system begins to malfunction, we'll start having feelings of anxiety such as a fast heartbeat, cold hands, and negative thoughts. Ultimately, this downward spiral—if not dealt with—will lead to depression. In a state of depression, what used to be logical is now illogical, and what used to be illogical is now logical. As I expressed in my suicide letter earlier in this book, it made sense to me that, if I took my life, my family would be better off. As I think about that now, that thought is totally illogical.

Suicide can follow depression, and suicide can come in many forms. It could be emotional, physical, relational, financial, mental, or professional. It doesn't necessarily have to be physical death.

It could be a divorce, two best friends not speaking to each other, two business partners splitting up, a church split, or athletes quitting teams.

Here's how this plays out.

As a person's gas tank begins to empty, he or she often will become controlling and manipulative. The person will gradually start pulling away because he or she doesn't want anyone to know what's really going on, continuing to project his or her ideal self to the outside world. After that control and manipulation gets far enough along, a person in this state will start convoluting communication. You can't quite get your hand around the truth with people who are in this condition.

The next thing that happens is they will start attacking and discrediting anyone who recognizes what's truly going on. The person who is trying to help—maybe a friend or a spouse—often will get completely rejected and decide to end the relationship. Or, the person going through it will completely pull away from the helper as with other relationships in life. You may have seen this happen with people around you. You may have had it happen to yourself. This clearly happened to me, and I am thankful to be able to help others with this now.

The only way to overcome this is to close that gap between the ideal self and the real self, restoring the person's strength and energy. Let's explore one way to help with this in case you're feeling that your gas tank is running low.

First, think about the things, foods, people, places, and activities that *fill* your tank. Write them down.

Now, make a list of those same types of things that *empty* your tank. You may find that you even have people in your life who you need to avoid. You may need to get rid of some activities.

As you continue this process, I encourage you to spend less time on what empties your tank and, instead, focus more time and energy on what fills your tank.

And if you are having thoughts of suicide, please go tell your doctor. I am telling you that there is hope on the other side of this. You are not alone even though it feels that way. Don't hang on to it. Get some help. Don't try to get through this on your own.

26

BUMPER BUDDIES

BECAUSE OF MY PRIDE that led me off the Road to Neverland, I didn't invite accountability from anyone to help me stay on track toward my vision, mission, and purpose. I needed someone I trusted enough to whom I could say, "I'm traveling a lot, and I'm feeling rejected at home by my wife. Because of this, I feel like I'm getting off track." I needed a *bumper buddy*.

A *bumper buddy* is someone who loves you enough to tell you when you're getting off track and to bump you back on the right track. It's also someone you trust enough to tell when you feel like you're heading off the road to one of your Neverlands. (Feel free to use "bumper *person*" if "bumper *buddy*" is not the right term for you.)

A good bumper buddy would have said to me, "Come on. Let's get this clear. You're gone all the time, and *you're* feeling rejected? Wise up. You're the one who's gone. You may be feeling rejected, but there's a good chance you're causing the rejection." This kind of accountability would have helped to bump me back on the right track and to stay in that place of not doing what I said that I would never do.

Let's assume I got back on the right track but gradually started falling off the road again and heading in the wrong direction. Consider the pain and damage I could have prevented if I had said to my bumper buddy, "There's this woman who I'm really attracted to. I don't know what to do about this."

A good bumper buddy would've said, "Stop traveling. Don't go there. Take your wife and your kids to your mom and dad's house. Go rekindle your marriage." That's what a good bumper buddy would do.

Now, I am surrounded by dozens of bumper buddies. In every city and country I visit, I have bumper buddies who I love and trust. There's nothing I can't share with them if I need to. And there's nothing they can't say to me if they feel in any way I am getting off the right track. And there is nothing I can't share with them if I feel that they are getting off track. Our relationships are based on love and trust.

Right now, make a list of the people in your life who could be good bumper buddies for you. Who are the friends who love you enough to tell you the truth? Who are the friends you trust enough to share the truth with of what is *really* going on? I would recommend that you select bumper buddies who understand critical concepts such as V.S.T.E.E.L.E., the social covenant, the W.A.D.E.L. model, T.F.A., V.P.M.O.S.A., dealing with anger, and understanding your self-identity. If you can't find people who understand the tools you've been learning in this book, consider using that as an opportunity to teach them.

Bumper buddies don't need to be perfect, but they do need to be people who are in your life such as your spouse, friends, family members, and coworkers. As you invite your bumper buddies into a deeper relationship with you, these relationships will grow as trust builds and as you allow these people to speak truth into you.

Nobody can stay on the Road to Neverland and fulfill their life's purpose without bumper buddies to help them. Don't try this alone. There's too much at stake. We can't reach our leadership potential alone. We need each other.

CONCLUSION

AS YOU APPLY THESE relational and transformational leadership tools and processes every day, they will become woven into your lifestyle. They will become a part of you. I encourage you to start using them today.

You will know that you are becoming a relactional leader when you walk with others in a place that no "transaction" can separate you. That does not mean that you might not work someplace else or play for another team, but it won't be because of a transaction within the relationship. You can stand on a firm foundation of relationship and look down both ends of the relationship continuum of highly relational people on one end and highly transactional people on the other end. You will find that neither will drive you crazy. You will have discovered a need for both in every organization or sphere in which you have influence. This will make you a truely *transformational leader* and give you greater influence in every organization or sphere of influence in which you live, work, or play.

I'll leave you with a summary of some tools and ingredients we've discussed. These are the ones that I would put into your leadership cake first. The more of these you use, the better your relationships will be. Better relationships lowers stress and anxiety, which leads to higher performance.

Social Covenant

1. Sit with a team member, your entire team, or your family, and ask this question: "When we're together, how do we want to treat one another?" Write down a list of words that describe how do you want to treat each other.

2. Ask this question: "How would we want to deal with it if one of us broke that agreement?" Or, "What process would we use to resolve the breaking of that agreement?"

How to Approach Someone

1. Humility
2. Pre-forgiveness
3. Love
4. Truth

Self-Evaluation

1. See it.
2. Own it.
3. Change.

T.F.A.

1. Change the thought.
2. Change the feeling.
3. Change the action.

Six-Step Apology

1. State the offense.
2. Acknowledge that you were wrong.
3. Apologize.
4. Ask for forgiveness.
5. Ask for accountability.
6. Ask if there's anything else.

The Discipline Process

1. The Off-the-Record Meeting
2. The First Recorded Meeting
3. The Second Recorded Meeting (success or ask questions again)
4. Success or consequences

Affirmations

1. Remove insincere phrases.
2. Make eye contact.
3. Make it about the other person. (Don't use flattery.)
4. Be honest.
5. Affirm the person directly.

S.L.O.W.E.R. Listening Model

S = Square up and be silent.
L = Lean into the conversation.
O = Maintain an open posture.
W = Be willing to be engaged.
E = Make eye contact.
R = Relax, respond, and repeat.

Email Etiquette

1. Don't read energy or emotion into emails.
2. Use a greeting in your emails.
3. Use the communication channel on which you want the person to respond.
4. Be careful about using bold or all caps.
5. Use a clear subject line.

6. If addressing several topics, use bullet points or numbering.
7. Keep conversations intact.
8. Limit sending carbon copy (Cc) or blind carbon copy (Bcc) emails.
9. Don't resolve conflict through email.
10. Avoid using words in the wrong context.
11. Ban cussing.

Seven-Step Process for Handling an Upset Person

1. Remain silent.
2. Remain silent.
3. Remain silent.
4. Thank the person for the feedback.
5. Repeat back to be sure you fully understand what the person is saying.
6. Make a commitment and follow up.
7. Make a commitment and follow up on the problem once you have all the details.

The W.A.D.E.L. Model for Effective Meetings

W = Welcome
A = Ask questions
D = Discussion
E = Empower
L = Launch

V.S.T.T.E.E.L.E. and Lead

V = Vision
S = Serve
T = Teach
T = Train
E = Equip
E = Empower
L = Let go
E = Evaluate

Five-Step Process for Removing the Constraints

1. Identify the biggest constraint.
2. Exploit the constraint.
3. Subordinate everything else.
4. Elevate the constraint.
5. Break the constraint.

Organizational Models

1. The Visionary Model
2. The Servant Leadership Model
3. The Functional Responsibility Model
4. The Relactional Model
5. The Continuous Improvement Model

The Five Stages of Team-Building

Stage 1: Visionary
Stage 2: Servant Leadership
Stage 3: Functional Responsibilities
Stage 4: Relactional
Stage 5: Continuous Improvement

V.P.M.O.S.A.: Our Mission in Life

V = Vision
P = Purpose
M = Mission
O = Objectives
S = Strategies
A = Actions

Bumper Buddies

1. People who love you enough to tell you if you are getting off track
2. People you trust enough to tell you if your mind or heart is wandering off track

Gas Tank Fillers and Emptiers

Fillers	Emptiers

ENDNOTES

[1] Oswald Chambers, *My Utmost for His Highest*, "The Uncritical Temper", https://utmost.org/classic/the-uncritical-temper-classic/

[2] Gary Chapman, *The Five Love Languages* (Chicago: Northfield Publishing, 2015).

[3] "The Learning Pyramid" by World Bank, https://siteresources.worldbank.org/DEVMARKETPLACE/Resources/Handout_TheLearningPyramid.pdf

[4] Eliyahu M. Goldratt, *Theory of Constraints* (Great Barrington, MA: North River Press).